A BRIEF COMMENTARY
ON THE
GOSPEL OF LUKE

by
John J. Kilgallen, S.J.

PAULIST PRESS
New York/Mahwah

Library of Congress Cataloging-in-Publication Data

Kilgallen, John J.
    A brief commentary on the Gospel of Luke / by John J. Kilgallen.
      p.   cm.
    Bibliography: p.
    ISBN 0-8091-2928-0 (pbk.) :   (est.)
    1. Bible. N.T. Luke—Commentaries.   I. Bible. N.T. Luke.
II. Title.
BS2595.3.K54   1988
226'.4077—dc19   87-35973
                                                 CIP

Published by Paulist Press
997 Macarthur Blvd.
Mahwah, N.J. 07430

Printed and bound in the United States of America

Contents

iii

Contents

Contents

Introduction

In any Bible we pick up, we will always find the Gospel of Luke placed third among Gospels; on one side are the Gospels of Matthew and Mark, on the other is the Gospel of John. The location of Luke's Gospel in our Bible is logical. It is so like Matthew and Mark that it belongs with them, just as the three of them, so unlike John's Gospel, are separate from the Gospel of John. Within the first three Gospels, Matthew is always put first because for centuries in early Christianity it was considered the premiere Gospel, with Mark.being a summary or digest of Matthew. Luke's Gospel, then, is put third. John's Gospel, so unlike the other three, is put last because it is considered to have been written after the first three. The location of Luke's Gospel, then, is logical.

I give the above account of the positioning of Gospels in our Bibles only to emphasize the distortion that can arise by separating Luke's Gospel from Luke's Acts of the Apostles. By putting John's Gospel between Luke's Gospel and the Acts of the Apostles one might fail to realize a most important point, that Luke's two writings were intended by Luke to be read as two volumes of one work. In other words, the Gospel and the Acts complement each other; neither can be fully understood without the other. Luke wrote so that each work needed the other, because his understanding of reality was just like that: the life of Jesus was fully intelligible only by reading about the spread of God's word to the ends of the earth, and what was happening at the ends of the earth was intelligible only when one has read the life of Jesus of Nazareth.

That Luke saw such a tight unity between Gospel and Acts is reason for us to offer, not just a commentary or study of one or other of his works, but a book which stresses this unity so that one truly grasps Luke's peculiar vision and framework into which Gospel and Acts fit in a harmony. Indeed, my own hope in writing what I have written about Luke-Acts (the abbreviation commonly used for the Gospel of Luke and the Acts of the Apostles) is that I can show, by moving methodically through Gospel and Acts, just how Luke's vision was fleshed out. Because it took Luke two volumes to express himself (whereas it took Mark, Matthew, and John only one each to express himself), it is vital to understand why Luke was impelled to do things this way.

Let me be a bit more specific in speaking of this Lucan vision, even in this introduction. Luke's starting point is the religious experience of his own contemporaries. These are people, typified by Theophilus mentioned in Luke's introduction to Gospel and Acts, who are convinced that they will be saved from the powers of evil by commitment to God through Jesus of Nazareth. How peculiar this is, that people who never knew Jesus personally, who never knew Palestine, who were born after Jesus died, who never knew friends of Jesus—that these Romans and Turks and Greeks and Africans knew themselves to be saved by having called on the name of this Jesus! Who is this Jesus and how did the people of the 80's A.D. ever come to know him, the real him?

To explain to his contemporaries the events which led up to their commitments is the goal of Luke. To do this, Luke began with the singular events of the life of Jesus which reveal how powerful, wise, trustworthy the Lord really was. Integral to the truth about this Jesus is the demonstration that what Jesus did and said was anticipated by the Jewish Scriptures, for the plan to save was already detailed in those Scriptures and was waiting to be put into action by the coming of Jesus. But these very Scriptures, the expression of God's plan for salvation, spoke of God's wanting to save all mankind, beyond the life of the earthly Jesus. Thus, one cannot have done justice to God's plan by stopping the description of it at the departure of Jesus from this world. The plan goes on to its fullest completion, involving many in the movement of salvation beyond Palestine and beyond 30 A.D., beyond the marvelous life of Jesus. Jesus himself is seen as one, though the central, element in this plan; the offer of salvation extends beyond Jesus' time on earth. In fact, Luke so depicts things that Jesus is seen to continue his saving mission beyond his earthly life, as he directs and guides his apostles from Jerusalem to the ends of the earth.

It is this saving plan of God, spoken of so frequently in the Old Testament and put into action by Jesus, which at any given moment and place in history is directed by this same Jesus to all people till this age is replaced by the age to come. Theophilus and those like him, then, understand through Luke's writing just how the offer of salvation through Jesus was intended for them; they understand, too, who this Jesus is whom they confess to be their Lord; they see how he planned to have people represent him after his ascension and how he continued to direct them from his place at the right hand of the Father through the outpouring of the Holy Spirit. Clearly they see how the instructions they received were truly and accurately the instructions taught by Jesus, whether by word or by example.

The plan of salvation with Jesus as its essential part, then, is what Luke wanted to write about to his contemporaries. It took Luke two volumes to do this. Two separate volumes though they be, there is ample evidence that they should be read together. It is only fair, then, that my efforts to offer intelligent comments about Luke's work should highlight the unity of his two volumes; indeed, as it turns out, my main goal is to follow the thread of this unity through these two Lucan volumes, with a secondary goal of commenting on individual verses or sections of these works. Thus, even though my work comes in two volumes, it is not intended to be an exhaustive commentary on every line of Luke–Acts; I have preferred to offer comments on what I thought would be difficult problems in Luke's verses, on what I thought would help one understand the movement of Luke's thought and particularly the development of Luke's conviction about how the offer of salvation moved from Old Testament, through the Palestinian life of Jesus and then to the ends of the earth.

Since my concern is to stress the unity between Gospel and Acts which mirrors the unity between the earthly life of Jesus and all later times, it would probably be best and ideal if my own work were put into one, unified volume. Practical considerations, however, have directed otherwise, and so we have one volume dealing with the Gospel of Luke and a second volume dealing with the Acts of the Apostles. In so printing this work, we run the danger of Luke's own time when Gospel was written separately from Acts. I can only hope that physical division of my own work will not mislead the reader, that the reader will take up both of my volumes in an effort to see Luke's unity through to its completion.

With most writings about biblical books comes a number of introductory pages concerned about the times in which the biblical books were written, the identity of the biblical author and other interests of scholars generally through the centuries. All of this introductory material is given in my work in the first volume, before discussion of the actual biblical stories begins; this material is not repeated in the volume dealing with the Acts of the Apostles. It is my hope that my work, particularly with its careful attention to following the divine plan for salvation—from Jewish Scriptures, through Jesus' Palestine, to the ends of the earth—will help the reader situate himself or herself into this very same divine plan, that what Luke hoped to accomplish for his contemporaries will be accomplished for all of us who continue to read Luke and search in his writings for our own identities. May we see ever more clearly who we are and who He is who has brought, in so many and unexpected ways, the offer of salvation to our time.

SCHOLARSHIP AND LUKE–ACTS

What do the early traditions of Christianity have to say about the Gospel of Luke and the Acts of the Apostles? The earliest reference to the existence and worthiness of these two works occurs about 140 A.D. in the writings of a certain Marcion; from the way Marcion expresses himself, it is clear that Luke's Gospel and Acts were already highly valued among Christians.

Then, a fragment has remained of an otherwise lost document; this fragment, discovered by a Professor Muratori—and thus called the "Muratorian Fragment"—lists the Gospel of Luke and the Acts of the Apostles in such a way as to indicate that by the time of the writing of the Fragment (about 160 A.D.), the Gospel and Acts were considered special and revered books.

About 180 A.D. St. Irenaeus, the famous bishop of Lyons, France, claimed that the author of the Gospel and Acts was a companion of St. Paul; after Irenaeus's time, it was traditional to refer to the Gospel and Acts as the Gospel and Acts of Luke, a companion of Paul.

When Irenaeus said that the author of the third Gospel and of Acts was Luke, a companion of Paul, we presume that he concluded to this companionship from a study of Paul's own letters; given that so much of the second half of Acts has Paul at its center and that the author of Acts seems to identify himself with certain sections of Acts by the use of the first person plural pronoun "we," Irenaeus would have used the following statements to draw the conclusion that Paul and the author of Acts was Luke, a companion of Paul:

"Greetings from my dear friend, Luke, the doctor" (Col 4:14).

"Epaphras sends greetings; so does... Luke" (Phlm 24).

"Only Luke is with me" (2 Tim 4:11).

Since all three of these statements were recognized by Irenaeus to have come from letters Paul wrote in his last years on earth, the Luke he mentions is presumed to have been a part of much of Paul's later life, and therefore qualified to report about most all facets of Paul's work for Christ, including even that which Paul did in Rome.

Marcion, the Muratorian Fragment, Irenaeus—such are the earliest witnesses to the tradition about the revered existence and the authorship of the Gospel and Acts of the Apostles.

How should we evaluate this evidence? I suggest that we look to one other witness who, because of his authority and integrity and ability to put all the elements of tradition together, presents an excellent paragraph to study.

Eusebius, a Christian who eventually became a bishop, lived from 264 to 349 A.D. Student, scholar, and Bishop of Caesarea where Christian scholarship was noteworthy, where earlier Paul was imprisoned before the final voyage of his life and where still earlier, Peter had been freed from jail by an angel, Eusebius has left behind a multi-volume work called *Ecclesiastical History*, in which we find the results of his study about many Christian traditions. It is his paragraph about the Gospel of Luke and Acts of the Apostles which captures our attention now.

> Luke, who was by race an Antiochian and a physician by profession, was long a companion of Paul, and had careful conversation with the other Apostles, and in two books left us examples of the medicine for souls which he had gained from them— the Gospel, which he testifies that he had planned according to the tradition received by him from those who were from the beginning, and the Acts of the Apostles, which he composed no longer on the evidence of hearing but of his own eyes. And they say that Paul was actually accustomed to quote from Luke's Gospel, since when writing of some Gospel as his own he used to say "According to my Gospel" (H.C. Kee 177–78).

What does modern scholarship have to say in regard to what Eusebius, the historian, has handed on to us?

First of all, we must recognize both the strength and possible weakness of Eusebius' testimony. As to his strength, his words are based on the best possible research available to a person who was serious, honest and bright; he depended heavily on those oral remembrances which an older generation had learned from those others who had learned from still others who learned from the apostles' generation. As to possible weakness, Eusebius could not, as far as we can tell, get behind the traditions developed by the first century and later Christians, and thus could not verify those traditions as expertly and as scientifically as he—and we—would have liked.

As we move on to modern evaluations of the Eusebian paragraph, we should apply here what is applicable in most every discussion of material dealing with the Bible: on every point asserted by Eusebius there is disagreement with him, and among those who disagree with Eusebius opinions on just how to disagree with Eusebius are many—and among scholars there are those who often agree with Eusebius, too.

Many scholars are willing to accept Eusebius' statement that Luke was from Antioch; this implies for some that Luke was semitic by race, though not Jewish. A number of scholars are still willing to think of Luke as a physician, though the argument has been well made that Luke's knowledge of a human being's physical make-up is not really different from what any well-educated person of his generation, physician or not, would know. Many scholars are still willing to accept the idea that Luke was a companion of Paul, at least for some periods of his missionary life, even though the Acts of the Apostles reveals little knowledge of or concern for some of the fundamental Pauline teachings (e.g., mystical body, Jesus' death as redemptive death, the distinction of salvation by works from salvation in Jesus) and it is quite possible that the Luke of Paul's letters is not the Luke associated with the Gospel and the Acts of the Apostles.

Most scholars today agree that the author of the Gospel of Luke is the author of the Acts of the Apostles; they argue this from the likeness of style within the two works and from certain evident references by the Gospel to Acts and by Acts to the Gospel. Most scholars go further to say that the Gospel and Acts are two volumes of one work. This is not to say that they are thought to have been written one right after the other, but it does mean to say that one over-arching concept unites the two works in such a way that neither is completely understood, as far as the author is concerned, without reference to the other—and that this interlinking of the two works was intentional. Most scholars will also accept the tradition that the author of the Gospel and of Acts is named Luke. It should not be surprising, however, that some scholars are not convinced or even actively oppose the claims that the author's name must be Luke, that one person is responsible for the Gospel and Acts, that this person had the intention that the two works complement and complete each other, and that the internal and literary evidence argues that one person wrote both volumes.

Scholars accept the purpose Eusebius gives as Luke's reason for writing the Gospel and Acts; actually, what Eusebius gives is taken right from the first lines of Luke's Gospel, so scholars would not disagree with Eusebius' statement in this matter. Scholars do, however, disagree about the sources Eusebius says Luke used. Very few scholars would agree that Luke drew his stories, for his Gospel or for parts of Acts, from "conversation with the other apostles." Many will agree to accept Paul's influence on Luke as regards certain stories in the Acts of the Apostles. Many scholars accept the claim that Luke was an eye-witness to certain events of Acts, but certainly not to all of the events Acts narrates. If, for many, Paul was not a bountiful source of material for Luke's writing of Acts, and if Luke himself was an eye-witness only to some of the events he narrates, and if there is little confidence that Paul or other apostles were the sources for the Gospel stories, what do scholars say were the sources for the bulk of Luke's writing?

Let us consider the Acts of the Apostles first. A number of scholars have disputed any claims to certainty about sources for the first twelve chapters of Acts, those chapters which deal with Jerusalem, Judaea and Samaria in Palestine, with the earliest decade or two of Christianity, and with the

deeds of Peter, Stephen and Philip. This is a particularly dis-
couraging dispute, because what for centuries were thought
to be the earliest preachings of the apostles are now considered by many to be by-and-large the constructions of
Luke, even if some of the ideas and terminology of the
speeches go back to those who gave the speeches. As for
chapters 13–28, many scholars see much of the mind and
imagination of Luke as having worked prodigiously on details and stories and speeches handed down to Luke; perhaps
Luke was an eye-witness to parts of this chain of Acts stories,
particularly where he uses the first person plural "we" in his
story-telling, and perhaps he had traveled with Paul and had
at least a list of places and people, even a diary, dealing with
Paul's preachings—but all of this is so reworked and deftly
written that we cannot really separate out what Luke learned
from others and what he himself is contributing, from his
experience or from his imagination, to chapters 13–28.

May I repeat that scholars are divided on all these matters; many would like to be satisfied with the claim that,
though we cannot identify sources for Acts, we can be con-
fident that the stories of Acts are based on solid fact and
tradition rather than on the fancy and imagination of an un-
trustworthy and carefree "person called Luke." The study of
many scholars does yield this degree of security.

What do scholars consider to be the sources Luke used
to write his Gospel? A number of scholars are willing to
follow the ancient conviction, taught by St. Augustine and
worked out more fully in the last century by a professor
named Griesbach, that Matthew's Gospel is the basis of
Luke's Gospel; where Matthew clearly is not responsible for
Lucan material, they suggest other sources gathered under
the general heading of special Lucan material.

A second group of scholars follow a very popular theory
developed over the last two centuries, that Mark is the major

source for Luke (and for Matthew), and that, if Mark cannot account for all of Luke, one must look to other sources. These "other sources" are divided into two groups: first, there is a source called Q, which accounts for material common to Luke and Matthew while absent from Mark, and then there is a source, or a group of sources, from which Luke drew called Special Lucan material. Thus, in this opinion, Luke depends not on Matthew, but on Mark and Q—together with Special Lucan material.

Finally, a number of scholars prefer to avoid both the Griesbachian theory and the Marcan/Q theory and fashion some sources for Luke out of "early and trustworthy" witnesses, like Paul and Mary and Jesus' relatives, much as Eusebius suggested in his reference to "the other apostles" as some of Luke's sources. The fact that we can point to three theories of sources for Luke's Gospel reveals how modern scholarship has felt about Eusebius' suggestions, and shows also that no one theory has pleased the world of scholarship. On the basis of educated guessing, one would say that the Marcan/Q theory is the theory upon which the majority of scholars today depend in their attempt to understand Luke in the light of his "sources."

To finish our comments on Eusebius' paragraph, we should say that very, very few scholars today would agree that "Paul was accustomed to quote from Luke's Gospel." It is true, as Eusebius notes, that Paul occasionally refers to "my Gospel," but it is rather clear today that, though Paul's Gospel is not totally different from Luke's, there are enough differences between them to say that Paul did not draw his Gospel from Luke, nor Luke from Paul. Particularly is it true that Paul's presentation of Jesus is significantly different from Luke's. I should add that a formidable difficulty which makes Eusebius' claim of Pauline dependence on Luke an impossibility is the scholarly claim today that all of Paul's writings were completed and Paul was dead (67 A.D.) before Luke wrote his Gospel and Acts (about 80–85 A.D.).

Scholarship today, then, is not in total agreement with the Eusebian assessment of Luke and his writings; yet, the disagreements do not eliminate certain agreements still serving the Christian community some sixteen hundred years after the writing of Eusebius.

Thus far, we have learned something about Luke and his work through the study of statements about the Gospel and Acts and their author. Can we so study the Gospel and Acts as to tell us something else, something about the world of Luke, about the "context" in which Luke operated? Let us, as part of our introduction to the Lucan works, spend a few moments reflecting on "the world of Luke—Acts."

THE WORLD OF LUKE–ACTS

One way of describing a "world" is to note its physical aspects. For instance, Israel, the first scene of the Luke-Acts story, is only twenty miles wide at its narrowest and fifty miles wide at its broadest, being about one hundred twenty miles in length; this means that Israel would fit into less than one-fifth of Illinois. To fly from Jerusalem to Rome is to fly about nine hundred miles, and it is from Jerusalem to Rome that Luke takes us in his two volumes, though the journey from one city to the other is not as direct as nine hundred miles suggests. A major city like Jerusalem held about thirty-five thousand inhabitants. Antioch, the third greatest city of the Roman Empire, was notably more populated, reaching at times nearly a million in number; in Antioch Christianity developed missionaries and here followers of Jesus were first dubbed "Christians." Rome, of course, was the largest city of the Empire, though its urban development did not reach its greatest size until after the time of Jesus and of Paul's arrival there.

Whereas a city like Jerusalem would be made up of religious Jews, cities like Corinth, Thessalonica, Ephesus—great port cities of their century—would be home to hundreds of thousands of people who were from all over the known world of the time. What united many of these people was economics, the search for and holding on to jobs. Their values and definitions of the world and of happiness were often determined not by where they now lived, but by where and from whom they or their ancestors came. In other words, though the influence of what we know as Greek and Roman cultures was far-reaching, there were other influences from such places as what is now present-day Iran that were often clashing with the worlds of classical Greece and Rome. This intermixing involved convictions about god(s), ethical conduct, afterlife, family worth, obligations to society, true happiness, individual status in society, what powers control a human being's life, the value of human life, and the source of evil and how it is to be overcome. Israel itself, despite its efforts to walk the straight and narrow in its relationship with Yahweh, had to come to terms with the powerful and influential way of approaching life which we today call "wisdom"—that approach which says that my problems are to be solved in the last analysis by the human mind.

There is, however, another way of describing the world of Luke–Acts than that briefly indicated above. This has to do with the factors which framed the questions the New Testament tries to answer. We are interested here, not only in the external sizes and shapes that determined the world of the first century A.D., but also in the problems Jesus and his followers perceived to be the essential problems of life and the answers these people posed. This was a part of their world with which they were occupied every day, for it was the question of human happiness which occupied them, and it was the answer to this question that they were convinced they were conveying. It is to this aspect of their world that we devote some pages now.

Within the framework of Luke-Acts, the first group of people we want to understand is the generation of Jesus. But to understand this group of religious-minded Jews, we must understand the thrust of the writings which so heavily influenced their lives and defined reality for them; therefore we will look at the Jewish Scriptures, or our Old Testament.

The Old Testament is made up of forty-six pieces of literature, a literature characterized by a great variety of poetry and prose. For all this variety and size the main subject matter is always the same. God exists; as such he imposes himself on all he creates and, as it is his love for others which gives them the happiest of lives, it is their love for him which allows him to actually bestow this happiness on them. Every page of the Jewish Scriptures somehow relates to this relationship of God and his creation, particularly human creation.

God's first effort to give human beings happiness was, according to the Jewish sages, what God did for Adam and Eve. That they were the parents of the entire human race shows that what God intended to give them he intended for all their children. Adam and Eve broke off their relationship with God and, in fact, brought evil to a world which from its creation had not known it. God then made Adam and Eve go their own way, out of his world into the human condition which we experience everyday. Here is seen for the first time the correlation between obedience to God and ultimate human happiness. There is no debate here about Adam and Eve enjoying various pleasures from life, whatever they might find or create for themselves. What is detailed here is the reason why, no matter what other joys one might find in life, one will no longer enjoy the fullness of happiness—

and with no hope of complete happiness, the little happiness along the way begins to turn sour. Happiness is receiving all God can give, but even this definition presupposes a relationship not only of receiving, but of giving—even if it be only a giving of obedience, of love. Adam and Eve, and their children, failed to give this.

God had mercy on Adam and Eve to the extent that he did not destroy them for their challenge to the Almighty God. But eventually he did rid himself of the evil offspring of Adam and Eve, except for Noah. With Noah and his family God began again. Yet, within a short number of generations, the descendants of Noah were a disappointment to God. At this point God embarked on a third plan—not creating all anew as with Adam or with Noah, but focusing on one people among the many people of the earth. God would found a people who would be so admirable that the rest of the world would be moved to live like this people, to worship its God, to find its happiness in this God. This people would be a light for the rest of the world in darkness. This people would, God decided, descend from Abraham.

As with Adam and Eve and with Noah, there was a formidable miracle in Abraham's case: God made sure that Abraham and Sarah, who in human estimation could not have a child, did have a child. Thus, divine intervention is at the very root of Israel. And that divine power and love intervened continually for the preservation and development of the people who should be the light of the world. God blessed Isaac and Jacob and saved Jacob's children from famine by preserving their brother Joseph in Egypt until the time he could be their provider.

God raised up Moses to save his people, and, though they often rebelled against him, shared with them his mind about human existence (this is the law of Moses) and brought this people into the land promised to Abraham. God fought on their side through mighty men and women called judges so that Israel would be protected. He gave them greatest rulers like Saul and David and Solomon; with the reign of Solomon Israel had blossomed immeasurably in comparison to that small beginning with Isaac and Jacob. At this time, Israel was a major power in its part of the world, and it was so through the constant help of Yahweh.

Now, Israel had not always and in every way remained obedient to Yahweh; the forty years in the desert had shown how recalcitrant Israel could be. But into the reign of Solomon the balance showed an Israel which was cooperative with God to the point that God showered his protection and love upon Abraham's children. All this changed, however, with the death of Solomon.

Solomon was Israel's most prestigious king, but he committed a sin which assured the destruction of his kingdom. In an attempt to solidify relationships with surrounding powers, Solomon had married a number of foreign women. To please them he had built temples in which these women, and their entourages, could worship their own gods—and he did this in Jerusalem, within sight of the temple of the only true God. In short, Solomon cooperated in developing the worship of false gods; the punishment for this was the division of his kingdom at his death.

Solomon's sin had national consequences, for he as king represented his people before God. As he went, so went the nation. The successors of Solomon, over thirty-five kings in all who ruled the kingdom of the north (Israel or Samaria) and the kingdom of the south (Judah), proved in the main to be no benefactors to their subjects. Only two of these kings were judged "good" by Old Testament standards, i.e., by the criterion of how they obeyed the law of Yahweh; all others were either in part or wholly bad. God had intervened in the sense that he continually sent messengers, prophets, to warn these kings against their sins of idolatry and injustice: Elijah, Isaiah, Amos, Hosea, Jeremiah, Ezekiel. Rarely was any positive response given to these prophets, and so the more pessimistic became the messages they delivered.

Ultimately, the northern kingdom paid for its disobedience by exile at the hands of the Assyrians in 722 B.C.; few if any of the exiles were ever heard from again. Spared because Assyria simply wasn't interested in it enough to expend great energies, the southern kingdom continued to exist, but only till 587 B.C. Then the Babylonians captured the south, destroyed Jerusalem and the temple of God built there by Solomon, and took to Babylon all those who had not been fortunate enough to flee to Egypt. Sin had had its way with Israel and it had ended disastrously.

After the Persians defeated the Babylonians, they allowed to go back to Jerusalem those Jews who wanted to; it is now 538, about fifty years since the exile of the south. Many of those who returned did so out of religious motivation: here alone is the land and the place of the temple given by God, designated as theirs by God. It was this religious impulse which began to rebuild from the ashes the city of Jerusalem and a society centered on obedience to God. The law of God would be the law of the land. The temple of God would be rebuilt. Religious people would guide the people of Israel, and kingship would be an institution abandoned, for its evil had been the cause of Israel's terrible fate. It is this group of religious people who gathered into one "book" documents from various ages of Israel's development. These people edited all these documents written by their forefathers so that what was written in diverse places and at diverse times and by diverse Israelites should now hand down to future Jewish children the lesson learned from Israel's history: to obey God is the only way to sure and complete happiness, to disobey God is the sure way to lose any chance for the happiness for which every being longs.

We have not detailed all the history of Israel. On the other hand, we have had to provide at least an outline of it, for it is concrete events, and not just theory, which ultimately convinced Israelites, if only for a short while, about the relationship between obedience to God and human happiness. When one passed on to his children, and they to theirs, the Old Testament's teaching about love of God and human happiness, one was speaking from the hardness and bitterness of pain and death and from the joy and peace of success and prosperity. These realities are what made the message of the Old Testament convincing.

All that has been said so far about the lesson to be learned from Israel's history is meant to explain or make clear just why the central, all-engrossing concern of the New Testament generation of Jesus was teaching the will of God and motivating obedience to it. History had made it clear that all other matters were incapable of providing or ruining ultimate happiness; only one's relationship with God counted in the ultimate tally. The Jews of Jesus' time, very practical people, paid thorough attention to what determined final, complete and full happiness or its opposite.

What happens in the New Testament times of Jesus is more properly divided into three concerns, resulting from what Jesus' generation had been taught by their forefathers. First, because of Jesus' ingenuity, there was a further stirring of waters already stirred by such people as Sadducees, Pharisees, and Essenes; everyone agreed that the will of God was to be obeyed, but what precisely was the will of God? Thus, we find in the Gospels a constant tension about interpretation of God's will; indeed, Jesus so upset traditional understandings of God's will that he was judged worthy of death, for he was tampering with nothing less than Israel's way to ultimate happiness.

Second, there is a concern in the Gospels to motivate people to "convert," to "repent," to "return" to the God of their forefathers and to his will. Jesus, John and others were concerned not only with interpreting the will of God, but with moving people to obey it as well.

Third, along with the severe lessons that Israel's history taught Jesus' generation about human happiness, there is another strain developing and persisting in the Old Testament writings; at least later Jews claimed that this line of thinking was present in documents written even in the earliest stages of their history. This is the divine intervention—in the form of suggestions, images, promises—that whatever suffering Israel will undergo, Yahweh will remain faithful and eventually free Israel from its terrible punishments of exile and death to enjoy a new kingdom where there will be only joy and peace, because it will be a kingdom where God rules, not the enemies of Israel or those powers which frustrate and dominate human beings to their harm. It is a new kingdom offered at various times in Jewish history, even at Israel's lowest moments, which Jesus' generation has come to expect, to look for anxiously. There never was a sure way to calculate the kingdom's coming mathematically, nor was it altogether agreed upon as to just how this kingdom would look: for many, nothing less than a totally new creation would really do justice to the concept of "the kingdom of God." Whatever the different forms that people imaged God's kingdom to be, they agreed that it was coming and were poised to listen carefully and to watch concernedly for any signs that "now" is the time.

For this reason two more characteristics of the New Testament become better understood. First, some had concluded over many decades and centuries that someone would appear on behalf of God to ring in God's kingdom—someone would be anointed to do this. Second, repentance took on a more precise meaning: one was not simply repenting in order to become true to one's calling as a chosen one of Yahweh, but one was repenting in order now to be worthy to enter the kingdom at hand. Only those worthy of God would enter into that world where God alone was king, where God alone bestowed blessings.

Israel's history, then, had contributed enormously to the make-up of Jesus and his generation. In short, those who took God seriously were concerned with three things: understanding God's law, obeying God's law, preparing for his kingdom. Historical events—reality—had created these concerns; it is these three things which dominate Jesus' world.

THE WORLD AFTER JESUS DIED

Jesus died, then rose from the dead to sit at the right hand of his Father. The Gospels differ on precisely what the disciples did after Jesus' resurrection. Mark's Gospel indicates that the Twelve were to return to Galilee to meet the risen Jesus; Matthew's Gospel notes that they actually went to Galilee for this encounter. John's Gospel also pictures the disciples as returning to their fishing nets in Galilee and there having some memorable experiences with Jesus.

It is Luke's Gospel and the Acts of the Apostles which describe the disciples centered around the Twelve, in company with Mary and Jesus' family, staying in Jerusalem until the outpouring of the Holy Spirit. Indeed, they were commanded by Jesus to await this outpouring and to begin their witnessing to him—in Jerusalem. It is not altogether clear how the various Gospel accounts can be brought into harmony as regards the post-resurrection period as it affected the disciples. Luke is clear, however, in beginning the witnessing to Jesus in the Holy City which crucified Jesus.

What form did this first witness in Jerusalem take? If, as many interpreters suggest, we cannot be sure of what elements of the early speeches in Acts are really historical, were actually spoken in the first days and years after Jesus' ascension we then have no clear and precise information about how converts to Christianity were made in these earliest times in Jerusalem. We do know, nonetheless, from remarks St. Paul makes in his Letter to the Galatians some twenty-five years after Jesus' ascension that he had met, around 42 A.D., leaders of the Jerusalem church. Though Paul does not describe this Jerusalem community, not even to indicate its size, we can be sure that it began shortly after Jesus' ascension, with many of its members being disciples of Jesus himself.

Precisely how new members came to be added to the already existing community is not, we acknowledge, clear. Yet, we cannot underestimate the influence of actual discussions with potential believers about how Jesus fulfilled the expectations of the Jewish Scriptures. If there was one persistent catechetical and missionary method, it was the constant intertwining of the Old Testament with the Jesus experience, whereby one made sense of Jesus and Jesus satisfactorily completed mysterious sayings and hopes expressed through the ages of God's communications with Israel.

We know that a stage of diversity was reached in the Jerusalem community soon after Jesus' ascension. Jews who had lived most of their lives outside Palestine, and were recent arrivals in Jerusalem, now became followers of Jesus. Though it is difficult to detail how these diaspora Jews-become-Christians differed from Jewish Christians who lived their whole lives in Palestine, it is clear that the two groups were recognizably different—even though Jewish in origin and now Christian in belief. One particularly significant dis-

tinction between these two groups of Jewish Christians was
their attitudes toward the temple of Jerusalem and toward
the Jewish law. Whereas the Jewish Christians who had followed Jesus and were native to Palestine had a respect and
reverence for the temple and the law very similar to the
non-Christian Jews of Jerusalem and Palestine, the non-native Christian Jews were much more willing to look on the
temple and certain elements of the traditional law as "secondary" and thus replaceable with a more profound vision.

This difference in attitude regarding temple and law ultimately led to a persecution of non-native Jewish Christians.
This persecution was severe enough to drive the persecuted
out of Jerusalem into greater Judea and Samaria, and well
beyond all of Palestine. The irony of this oppression was
that, while certainly ridding itself of Christian Jews perceived as antagonistic to Jewish traditions, Jerusalem was
providing witness to Jesus to other territories—Cyprus,
Phoenicia, Syria and, eventually, to the ends of the world.

A center for Christianity grew up out of this dispersal
of Christians: the church of Antioch, in Syria, become vi-
brant. Some scholars consider Antioch to be a second Jerusalem because of its inner energetic Christian life;
moreover, Antioch became known for its eagerness to look
beyond itself to other cities, other shores, other lands. Further, Antioch developed a certain tolerance which made
eventual baptism of Gentiles, who previously had known or
practiced nothing of Judaism, a baptism without circumcision or other Jewish customs traditionally thought necessary
for salvation. It is improbable that the majority of leading
Jewish Christians in Jerusalem would have welcomed Gentiles so gladly under these conditions.

From Antioch, then, sprang the desires of Paul and Barnabas, and others too, to bring the name of Jesus throughout
their world. For Paul, this "world" initially meant territories

not too far from his native Tarsus, e.g., Derbe, Iconium, Cyprus. But little by little, under divine guidance, Paul and others worked ever outward and developed Christian communities eventually in most of present-day Turkey, Macedonia, Greece and Rome.

The immense varieties of peoples that Christian preachers met and converted is a reality we must be conscious of, at least for the reason that this variety forced upon the Christians a new way of presenting Jesus and the will of God. To a Palestinian Jew it meant everything to say that the Messiah, the Son of David, was within his reach. But to a Greek, Messiah and Son of David were terms which carried no value. To keep these terms, one would have to teach the Greek the Jewish way to understanding reality before the Greek could grasp the place and importance of Messiah and Son of David. On the other hand, there were existing symbols of value in Greek society by which the worth of Jesus could be expressed, e.g., Lord, Benefactor, Redeemer, Judge; Jesus, then, would be redescribed, redressed as it were, so as to be recognizable as a value to a Greek. What was done for a Greek, of course, was then done for a Macedonian, a Roman, an Ephesian. This attention to the variety of audiences Christian preachers met does not obscure the fact that missionaries, whose practice was to start in the synagogue of a new town, appealed first to Jews—and used as a primary tool the ever authoritative Jewish Scriptures. One can catch a glimpse of the fruit of this persistent linking of Jesus and the Old Testament in the pervasive presence of Old Testament texts and imagery in all New Testament writings, particularly in the Gospels.

As the preaching about Jesus spread over the Mediterranean basin, Christian preachers had to be ready for new ways of thinking, new emphases about Jesus. Perhaps two examples drawn from Acts will suffice to show this feature of the middle first century A.D. In Lystra, Paul and Barnabas are automatically considered nothing less than gods because of the miracles they worked there; no Jew would have ever made such a mistake—for the Jew there was only one God. In Athens, Jesus was best kept to the middle or end of Paul's missionary speech; first, agreement had to be reached about the reality of God and his expectation that human beings would lead lives that merited happiness, and only after this agreement could Jesus be identified as the one who will judge who indeed deserves happiness. Such are only two examples of the newness of the worlds that a person like Paul had to master. The world in which he spent the last fifteen or twenty years of his life was strikingly different from earlier Jewish years. But what was true for him as an individual eventually became a corporate characteristic: Christianity obliged itself to adjust to new circumstances as it sought to give its message to new kinds of people.

Through all the diversities of cultures and values and definitions about life's meaning, there does surely run one constant thread which we must think about. No matter what the diversity, many individuals had some kind of experience of salvation by calling on the name of Jesus. I say "some kind of experience" because no one really details for us just what moved people to find their salvation in Jesus, what brought about in them the conviction that they were saved through him. But Romans and Macedonians and Colossians and Corinthians all attest to the Lordship of Jesus and profess that they are, through him, saved people. Indeed, the sense of being saved by Jesus, as it spread throughout the Mediterranean, is quite analogous to the awareness of physical healing of Palestinian Jews. Physical healing is a good way of trying to describe the saving of people on the deeper, fuller level of the spirit.

AND HERE ENTERS LUKE

Luke knew in depth the worlds of Jesus and of the greater Mediterranean which we have briefly discussed. Watching the development of Christian communities and hearing the persistent conviction that Jesus alone was Lord and Savior, Luke perceived the unity which existed between Jesus and people who never met Jesus, never knew Palestine, lived generations after Jesus and were not Jewish in background. He saw further that this unity extended to the heart of the Old Testament, for the Savior Jesus was foretold by God through the Jewish writings: he was the central part of God's plan to save all human beings. Luke, then, decided to show Christians of his time that what they experienced through calling on Jesus was really the flowering of a plan in existence from the beginning of time. They were not simply individuals, each with his private destiny, but they were also to find their identity through discovery of their relationship to the historical Jesus and to the Old Testament, all of which takes one into the very mind and intention of God.

The Gospel of Luke, written with a concern for the people of the 80's A.D., presents Jesus, then, as the flowering of a long-made plan of God to save everyone. Organically, Jesus proceeds from the Jewish Scriptures. But it is not enough to present, as Mark and others had done, the true meaning of Jesus of Nazareth. Luke had to show that the thrust of the divine plan continues beyond the public life of Jesus of Nazareth to every time and every place, with Jesus the Lord to be called upon for salvation. Organically, the preaching and conviction of being saved is the fuller flowering of the same divine plan which prepared for the historical Jesus of Nazareth. It is the plan, then, which Luke sets out to describe when he links his Gospel to Acts; it is the experience of the 80's A.D. which Luke wishes to ground properly for converts linked with Jesus, but ignorant of his time, his place, his humanity.

Luke's goal, then, is to describe the flowering of God's saving plan. To this goal is added a second: whatever will help solidify the teachings his audience has received about Jesus and about the way of life God has asked for through Jesus—whatever will help solidify and strengthen belief—this is what Luke will write. He will tell the Jesus story, then, and that of the apostles in such a way that one will come away more convinced than ever of the rightness of his commitment, more satisfied with his dedication to Jesus. We should not, therefore, think of Luke as unconcerned about historical facts; he does his best to base his writings on them. But his goal in writing indicates that he wants the reader to come away, not with a book dedicated simply to historical facts, but with assurance, confidence, full trust in the commitments he has made to Jesus as his Lord.

It is this saving plan of God which makes the Gospel and Acts into one book with two volumes. Perhaps it is better to say that the need of 80 A.D., the need to see clearly and comfortingly how an individual is rooted in the divine eagerness and plan for his salvation, gives impetus to the spelling out of just how a person of the 80's A.D. is linked in time and space to Jesus, and through him to God.

In describing the details of this plan, Luke liberally conveys to his reader the sense of Jesus' teaching, a teaching as applicable in the 80's as it was in 27 A.D. Moreover, he makes sure that the Lord Jesus serves as model for the believer's life with God. Finally, he so presents the power of Jesus that one can only rejoice to think that this power will be lovingly expended on one's own person. Though Palestinian Jews had interpreted Jesus as the one to inaugurate a new heaven and a new earth, a newness which he did not in fact initiate, the power and wisdom and goodness of Jesus

of Nazareth offers a momentary enjoyment of God's kingdom. This contact was temporary, but will become perma-
nent in due time. Till then, the Savior continues his search
for commitment to himself, for belief in himself, as the way
to complete happiness.

The Spirit of God, promised for the end of time, has
been given and operates lavishly through the world. That
this gift, which is the culmination of Jesus' earthly career of
27–28 A.D., was given to people who had never practiced
the Jewish religion invited Jewish Christians to the realization that a new way of relating to God is in operation. God
can offer salvation to those who have had nothing to do
with Judaism. The centrality of Jesus is underlined now in
a spectacular way and the subordination of God's law to
Jesus is a logical consequence of his being the only door to
salvation. God showed the way in this revolution of man's
understanding of what was necessary for salvation; man
could never have changed this understanding on his own.
God, however, gave salvation to Gentiles without circumcision and did not allow them to think that obedience to
the law, without faith in Jesus, would be saving. Indeed, by
putting Jesus ahead of all else, Jesus becomes the source by
which we learn whether any law is required of us for salvation. The commitment to him, then, is the way God has
chosen for the salvation of mankind. It falls to Luke to explain all of this to his contemporaries, and through this ex-
plaining he will strengthen and deepen commitment to the
Lord.

It is with these introductory remarks that we begin our
reflections on Luke's Gospel and Acts. Our interest is to reveal the unity of the story Luke tells, but while doing this
we hope to underline the many other central thoughts Luke
expresses in each of his chapters. May we readers today be
rewarded with the comfort and deepening of faith for which

Luke wrote his works so long ago, and may the comments we make about Luke's work be a help to this comforting and deepening of faith in Jesus, Lord and Savior.

1

THE GOSPEL: VERSES 1–4

Verses Which Serve To Introduce Both the Gospel and the Acts of the Apostles

As a brief look at this entire book will show, I have divided my comments according to the chapter divisions already existent in Luke's works. That I follow a different scheme in regard to Luke's first Gospel chapter underlines the fact that he, and we, recognize a distinction of great importance between the first four verses of Chapter 1 and all the other verses of the same chapter. Verses 1–4 serve, in short to introduce the entire Lucan work, both Gospel and Acts. They deserve separate and careful attention.

In some Bibles the first four verses of Luke's Gospel comprise at least two sentences, but it is noteworthy that, when Luke wrote the material covered by these four verses, he wrote it all as one, and only one, sentence. A sentence of such length, when it is written with grace and good style, reveals that its author is an educated man, capable of sustaining a pleasing classical style of writing if he so wishes. Thus, the very first sentence of Luke's Gospel introduces us to the kind of person we have for our author.

But the sentence embraced in four verses is the only one of its stylistic kind in the entire Lucan writings; nowhere else do we see such quality writing. We might, then, conclude that this isolated sentence is a literary fluke, but scholars do not think it to be such. Rather, scholars understand Luke's different styles of writing as signs of his ability to adjust his literary style to the circumstances which he wants to describe. To be specific, Luke's first two Gospel chapters

SCRIPTURE TEXT

1 Inasmuch as many have undertaken to compile a narrative of the things which have been accomplished among us, ²just as they were delivered to us by those who from the beginning were eyewitnesses and ministers of the word, ³it seemed good to me also, having followed all things closely for some time past, to write an orderly account for you, most excellent Theophilus, ⁴that you may know the truth concerning the things of which you have been informed.

(excluding verses 1–4 of Chapter 1) are notably akin in style to the style in which the Greek version of the Old Testament (called the Septuagint) is written. Scholars conclude that Luke wrote his introductory sentence in classical Greek style because he wanted to catch the eye of his educated contemporaries, but switched to the biblical Greek style of the Old Testament as a subtle way of linking the pre-adult stories of Jesus and John with the Old Testament, as though they emerged naturally from the Old Testament, in the style of the Old Testament. Thus, Luke not only hopes that his reader will see how Jesus and John in their earliest years correspond to the expectations and hopes of the Old Testament; he so writes up their earliest days as to make one think he is still in, or only emerging from, Old Testament times. Even style is used to express Luke's conviction that Jesus is naturally the culmination and fulfillment of the Jewish Scriptures.

Together with the observation about the style of the first four verses are some pertinent observations about individual elements of the verses.

Luke speaks of "many others" who had undertaken to write accounts of Christian events. Who these many others may be is, unfortunately, not known; perhaps Luke is referring to Mark and other authors whose works he has used in preparing his own Gospel and Acts. Whoever "they" actually are, notice of them lets us imagine to a greater degree than otherwise what kinds of enthusiasm had already existed before Luke in trying to make sense, indeed through writing, of the great events of first century Christianity. In our Gospels we have only a fraction of what the early Christians, in longer or shorter writings, tried to put together as a coherent description of Jesus' life and the lives of those who followed him. We have here in Luke's first line a hint of activity which intrigues us.

These "many others" have attempted to draw up accounts. Such a phrasing as "draw up accounts" suggests the written word, something beyond just oral expression. Since the majority of scholars believe that Luke never saw Matthew's Gospel or John's Gospel, we can only imagine the kinds of work to which Luke refers; for all that, his witness that many had tried what he was doing, that he was one among many before him, is a revealing piece of information.

The "events which have come to completion among us" do not, for some scholars, include the events described in the Acts of the Apostles; the clause refers only to Gospel events. This scholarly opinion is questioned by many other professionals who see in this Lucan reference a witness that early Christians tried to link together both the Gospel stories and stories of post-Gospel activity. But even if the words "events which have come to completion among us" refer only to stories about Jesus, we are to note that these Jesus-events have their completion "among us," that is, in Luke's own time of 80 A.D. Such a way of describing these "events" is very important, for it expresses the insight that what happened in Jesus' life has its fulfillment and reaches its completion only many years after Jesus' life on earth is over.

Luke does not specify exactly why events of Jesus' life are completed only in later generations, but he has revealed enough to let us know how tightly interwoven he sees the events of Nazareth, Galilee and Jerusalem and the conversions in Ephesus, Corinth and Rome.

Another important statement of Luke is his affirmation that the events handed down to later generations are handed down with care, without deviation from the care with which they were first formulated into stories. Luke affirms here that people who learned of the events of Jesus' life and of later events tried to remain faithful to what they had heard, tried to pass on the truths they themselves had received. Later

on, Luke will refer to his own efforts at honesty in research-
ing what he had received from others and in presenting the
meaning of Christianity's crucial events.

Luke then refers to "eyewitnesses and ministers of the
word." It seems best to understand Luke to mean that "eyewitnesses" were "ministers of the word." It is worth noting
that these "eyewitnesses-become-preachers of the word" are
distinctly of a different age than Luke and his contemporaries. Given other data, we think Luke is refering to a difference of almost fifty years between his audience and the
audiences of the first ministers of the word.

Up to this point in his first sentence Luke has referred
to a number of others who have been active in what will
come to be known as Gospel writing; he has given us much
to ponder about early Christian times and endeavors. Now
Luke speaks about himself.

Luke first assures his reader that he has gone over the
entire story from the beginning. Such an assurance includes
both the admission that Luke himself was not an eyewitness
to most all of what he writes and the personal confirmation
that he carefully reviewed all that he had received. What
Luke has received has come from eyewitnesses and ministers of the word; yet, Luke has reviewed it all with care,
presumably so that he can honestly say that what he passes
on is the truth.

With this review done, Luke determines to put something in writing. What characterizes this writing is the order
into which Luke has put all his material. Though Luke does
not himself describe what kind of order he uses, it seems
clear from the study of what he has written that the order
is less interested in chronology for its own sake and much
more interested in how events can be lined up to reveal
best the plan of God in the life of Jesus and of those who
represented Jesus after his ascension. Luke's concern is not

the time or other circumstances of events, but the meaning of events, both in themselves and in relation to one another. To this end he fashions an order among the events as he writes them.

Theophilus is the designated recipient of Luke's work. Most scholars think Theophilus is the man who sponsors Luke's projected work, i.e., it is Theophilus who pays for the manuscript materials and for the publication of what Luke writes, as well as for making copies of Luke's work.

But Theophilus is also a Christian, a believer that Jesus is his Lord, his Savior and indeed the designated Lord and Savior of all men and women. Why is Luke writing his Gospel and Acts to Theophilus? Here we must follow Luke's thought very carefully. Luke's own words indicate that Theophilus has already been taught; it seems safe to say that this earlier "teaching" has accompanied Theophilus' entrance into the Christian community through baptism. Thus, Luke is not dealing with a beginner, or with someone who needs elemental teaching; all that is presumed. Rather, what Theophilus needs, Luke indicates, is such a presentation of the events of Jesus' life and of events after the ascension that Theophilus can see how well founded, how trustworthy, how sure was the teaching he had earlier received. What Luke is after, then, is confirmation of something already learned, sureness about what one has been taught. It is the presentation of stories in a certain way that will create this sureness, this confidence, this sense that what Theophilus had been taught is really trustworthy.

The Gospel and Acts, then, are supremely pastoral documents in their intention, for they are concerned with the well-being of Theophilus— and, we should say, of anyone who reads them as a believer. Is Luke interested in presenting facts? Yes, for facts can help one's confidence in what he has been taught. But he is more concerned to bring out the deepest meaning of events and words. Thus, Luke does ascertain facts, but he spends most all his energy in trying to show Theophilus the meaning of those facts. Luke's hope and presumption is that, after Theophilus lays down the full work of Luke, Theophilus will be more firmly convinced than ever that Jesus is Lord and Savior, and that he, Theophilus, is the logical flowering of the plan of God seeded throughout the entire Jewish Scriptures.

The initial sentence of Luke, its length spreading over four verses, tells us much about the purpose of Luke's writings, about the person to whom he writes, about the sources Luke depends on. For all this information we cherish this Lucan sentence very much.

THE GOSPEL: VERSES 5–80

Heaven Announces the Conceptions of John and Jesus • John Is Born, Raised in the Desert

In the temple chamber called "The Holy," a chamber next to the holiest space on earth—"The Holy of Holies," the private room of Yahweh—the angel Gabriel announces to Zechariah that he and his wife Elizabeth will have a son. Zechariah and Elizabeth are pious people, waiting in fidelity for the coming of God's kingdom. A miracle is announced to Zechariah: a son to be called John (= the Graciousness of Yahweh). The key element in this angelic visit is Gabriel's explanation of the role John will play in the plan of God for his people, for the very calm and assuredness of the angel shows that the Lord has a plan in mind. John is defined as one who comes to Israel in the power and spirit of Elijah, the ninth century B.C. prophet who struggled energetically to keep for Yahweh a people pleasing to him, a people worthy to stand in his presence. John will give external sign of his special dedication and role: like great heroes of Israel's past, John will abstain from wine, any strong drink. He will be a source of joy for so many who will be acceptable to God (and thus able to inherit his goodness and peace) if they follow the wisdom and exhortation of John. The angel's announcement, then, prepares the reader for the role John will play in Luke 3:1–18: he will try to prepare a people to stand worthily in the presence of the God who is coming.

Six months later, the same angel Gabriel brings notice of a second conception, of a further step in the divine plan. To Mary in Nazareth, some eighty miles north of the an-

5 In the days of Herod, king of Judea, there was a priest named Zechariah, of the division of Abijah; and he had a wife of the daughters of Aaron, and her name was Elizabeth. [6]And they were both righteous before God, walking in all the commandments and ordinances of the Lord blameless. [7]But they had no child, because Elizabeth was barren, and both were advanced in years.

8 Now while he was serving as priest before God when his division was on duty, [9]according to the custom of the priesthood, it fell to him by lot to enter the temple of the Lord and burn incense. [10]And the whole multitude of the people were praying outside at the hour of incense. [11]And there appeared to him an angel of the Lord standing on the right side of the altar of incense. [12]And Zechariah was troubled when he saw him, and fear fell upon him. [13]But the angel said to him, "Do not be afraid, Zechariah, for your prayer is heard, and your wife Elizabeth will bear you a son, and you shall call his name John.

[14]And you will have joy and gladness,
   and many will rejoice at his birth;
[15]for he will be great before the Lord,
   and he shall drink no wine nor strong drink,
   and he will be filled with the Holy Spirit,
   even from his mother's womb.
[16]And he will turn many of the sons of Israel to the
   Lord their God,
[17]and he will go before him in the spirit and
   power of Elijah,
   to turn the hearts of the fathers to the children,
   and the disobedient to the wisdom of the just,

to make ready for the Lord a people prepared." [18]And Zechariah said to the angel, "How shall I know this? For I am an old man, and my wife is advanced in years." [19]And the angel answered him, "I am Gabriel, who stand in the presence of God; and I was sent to speak to you, and to bring you this good news. [20]And behold, you will be silent and unable to speak until the day that these things come to pass, because you did not believe my words, which will be fulfilled in their time." [21]And the people were waiting for Zechariah, and they wondered at his delay in the temple. [22]And when he came out, he could not speak to them, and they perceived that he had seen a vision in the temple; and he made signs to them and remained dumb. [23]And when his time of service was ended, he went to his home.

24 After these days his wife Elizabeth conceived, and for five months she hid herself, saying, [25]"Thus the Lord has done to me in the days when he looked on me, to take away my reproach among men."

26 In the sixth month the angel Gabriel was sent from God to a city of Galilee named Nazareth, [27]to a virgin betrothed to a man whose name was Joseph, of the house of David; and the virgin's name was Mary. [28]And he came to her and said, "Hail, O favored one, the Lord is with you!" [29]But she was greatly troubled at the saying, and considered in her mind what sort of greeting this might be. [30]And the angel said to her, "Do not be afraid, Mary, for you have found favor with God. [31]And behold, you will conceive in your womb and bear a son, and you shall call his name Jesus.

[32]He will be great, and will be called the Son of
the Most High;
and the Lord God will give to him the throne of
his father David,

[33]and he will reign over the house of Jacob for
     ever;
and of his kingdom there will be no end."
[34]And Mary said to the angel, "How shall this be, since I
have no husband?" [35]And the angel said to her,
     "The Holy Spirit will come upon you,
     and the power of the Most High will overshadow
          you;
     therefore the child to be born will be called
          holy,
     the Son of God.
[36]And behold, your kinswoman Elizabeth in her old age
has also conceived a son; and this is the sixth month with
her who was called barren. [37]For with God nothing will
be impossible." [38]And Mary said, "Behold, I am the hand-
maid of the Lord; let it be to me according to your word."
And the angel departed from her.

    39 In those days Mary arose and went with haste
into the hill country, to a city of Judah, [40]and she entered
the house of Zechariah and greeted Elizabeth. [41]And
when Elizabeth heard the greeting of Mary, the babe
leaped in her womb; and Elizabeth was filled with the
Holy Spirit [42]and she exclaimed with a loud cry, "Blessed
are you among women, and blessed is the fruit of your
womb! [43]And why is this granted me, that the mother of
my Lord should come to me? [44]For behold, when the
voice of your greeting came to my ears, the babe in my
womb leaped for joy. [45]And blessed is she who believed
that there would be a fulfilment of what was spoken to
her from the Lord." [46]And Mary said,
     "My soul magnifies the Lord,
[47]and my spirit rejoices in God my Savior,
[48]for he has regarded the low estate of his
          handmaiden.

For behold, henceforth all generations will call
    me blessed;
[49]for he who is mighty has done great things for
    me,
    and holy is his name.
[50]And his mercy is on those who fear him
    from generation to generation.
[51]He has shown strength with his arm,
    he has scattered the proud in the imagination of
      their hearts,
[52]he has put down the mighty from their thrones,
    and exalted those of low degree;
[53]he has filled the hungry with good things,
    and the rich he has sent empty away.
[54]He has helped his servant Israel,
    in remembrance of his mercy,
[55]as he spoke to our fathers,
    to Abraham and to his posterity for ever."
[56]And Mary remained with her about three months, and
returned to her home.

57 Now the time came for Elizabeth to be delivered, and she gave birth to a son. [58]And her neighbors and
kinsfolk heard that the Lord had shown great mercy to
her, and they rejoiced with her. [59]And on the eighth day
they came to circumcise the child; and they would have
named him Zechariah after his father, [60]but his mother
said, "Not so; he shall be called John." [61]And they said to
her, "None of your kindred is called by this name." [62]And
they made signs to his father, inquiring what he would
have him called. [63]And he asked for a writing tablet, and
wrote, "His name is John." And they all marveled. [64]And
immediately his mouth was opened and his tongue
loosed, and he spoke, blessing God. [65]And fear came on
all their neighbors. And all these things were talked

about through all the hill country of Judea; [66]and all who heard them laid them up in their hearts, saying, "What then will this child be?" For the hand of the Lord was with him.

67 And his father Zechariah was filled with the Holy Spirit, and prophesied, saying,

[68]"Blessed be the Lord God of Israel,
  for he has visited and redeemed his people,
[69]and has raised up a horn of salvation for us
  in the house of his servant David,
[70]as he spoke by the mouth of his holy prophets
    from of old,
[71]that we should be saved from our enemies,
  and from the hand of all who hate us;
[72]to perform the mercy promised to our fathers,
  and to remember his holy covenant,
[73]the oath which he swore to our father Abraham,
    [74]to grant us
  that we, being delivered from the hand of our
    enemies,
  might serve him without fear,
[75]in holiness and righteousness before him all the
    days of our life.
[76]And you, child, will be called the prophet of the
    Most High;
  for you will go before the Lord to prepare his
    ways,
[77]to give knowledge of salvation to his people
  in the forgiveness of their sins,
[78]through the tender mercy of our God,
  when the day shall dawn upon us from on high
[79]to give light to those who sit in darkness and in
    the shadow of death,
  to guide our feet into the way of peace."

[80]And the child grew and became strong in spirit, and he was in the wilderness till the day of his manifestation to Israel.

nouncement to Zachary, Gabriel tells of God's desire that she be the mother of a child to be called Jesus (= God saves through him). The role this Jesus will play far exceeds the Elijah role of John; Jesus will rule, like David his forefather, over the people of Israel. Jesus, in fact, is the One promised to David, the One who would be Anointed (= Messiah, Christos) to perform a service for God's people— and that service is to be their king. In God's mind, kingship is service, for it is through the wisdom, power and fairness and love of the king that God will disperse all his gifts to his people.

Through the words of Gabriel the reader is helped to penetrate the meaning of Jesus even before Jesus himself does or says a thing. But Luke goes even further. Gabriel so explains the conception of Jesus that one can only conclude that God himself is at the very source, like a father, of Jesus' being. John was described as empowered with the Holy Spirit of God from his very conception, in order to be able to play his crucial role for God. Jesus, however, can only be explained by saying that the Holy Spirit of God gave Jesus his being and his character, as would a father. It is because of this relation of God and his Spirit to Jesus that Jesus deserves two descriptions popular among Christians of Luke's time: Son of God and Holy One.

It is through the divinely authorized words of Gabriel, then, that the reader is prepared for the person of Jesus who will dominate the Gospel and the Acts of the Apostles. Mary speaks for herself as she freely chooses to accept God's plan for her. But Mary is used by Luke to stand also for the entire body of the faithful, the Church, as it pledges obedience, even in matters not fully understood.

Gabriel's visit to Mary leads Mary to Elizabeth. In a highly artful way, Luke reveals the relationship of John to Jesus, of Elizabeth to Mary: Jesus is Elizabeth's Lord; Mary is Mother of her Lord. Already Jesus is recognized publicly as the One to whom one commits one's life: that is the meaning of identifying him as Lord. It is a joyful moment, for to find one's lord, the one to whom a person can commit himself fully without fear and with a sense of fulfillment, is a joyful experience.

That Elizabeth is able to call Jesus "Lord" is attributed, it seems, to the movement of John in Elizabeth's womb. One might argue that such a movement, if it occurred, need not be interpreted as an indication that the Lord is present. But all these stories are filled with the Christian convictions of the 80's A.D., that Jesus, particularly by virtue of his resurrection, is deserving of the title "Lord." With this conviction the infancy narratives are being written; it is in the light of this conviction that Elizabeth's reaction is deemed logical.

Mary's response to Elizabeth is filled with imagery drawn from the Old Testament. In reciting her poem, Mary represents both herself and that Israel which has been lowly, despised, poor at the hands of the proud of heart who are rich, cruel, and princely. She sees in her Son the reversal of Israel's humiliation over the many past centuries: now God will exert himself on behalf of those who fear him, who persevere in trust and obedience to him. In short, we are brought to realize, for the first time expressly, that Jesus will overcome those forces which cruelly dominate us and which we cannot, for all our wishing or effort, dominate. Jesus is Savior; he fulfills God's promise stretching all the way back to Abraham: Israel will one day be free, at peace, happy, glorious.

Quickly Luke changes scenes, bringing us to the naming of John eight days after his birth—and to the poetic hymn of Zechariah which Luke uses to further interpret the miracles of John and Jesus. In the first half of his hymn, Zechariah shows the relationship of Jesus to the history and hopes of his forefathers: again Jesus is interpreted as the completion of God's promises over centuries to his people. They will now be saved from fear, from the hands of their enemies—so that the very reason for Israel's being and her glory might come true: the service of the one and true God in holiness and virtue in his presence, forever.

If Jesus is the one who actually saves, John will so work as to help the people of Israel have an experience of salvation. He will encourage them to purify themselves, to make themselves ready and worthy of God; if they will listen to John, they will repent; following upon repentance is that forgiveness from God which is in its own way an experience of being saved from forces over which one has no control. Who, what, Zechariah asks, can save me from remaining dead as the result of my sins? Not I, for I can neither forgive my sins nor free myself from death's hold on me, once I fall into his clutches; left to myself, once I am dead, I am dead forever, the truest effect of my sins. To follow John's plea for a return to God, the Source of Life, is to escape darkness and the shadow of death, to put one's feet onto the road which leads only to peace, light, life.

Luke's last note to the reader is that John, once grown, moves to the desert (where there were other religious Jews and Jewish communities, e.g., Qumran) to await Luke's bringing John forward to play his role in the Gospel (Lk 3). It is at this point that we remind ourselves that, unlike Matthew and Mark and John who present John the Baptist only as an adult and only in his role as forerunner of Jesus, Luke has chosen to intertwine the Baptist and Jesus even from their very conceptions. Why is this?

John may be interpreted as the last of the Old Testament, as the completion of a period before the New Testament begins with Jesus. Yet, in two ways John belongs with Jesus, as much as he belongs with the Old, prior Testament—and not only because he was an actual contemporary of Jesus. First, the role of John should rightly end in an experience of salvation in God's forgiving those who repent; since, however, salvation is the goal of Jesus *par excellence*, there is reason to link John with Jesus, rather than dissociate the one from the other. Second, as Luke 3:1–20 will show, John's preaching included his teaching what were deeds consonant with repentance, deeds which were befitting true sorrow for sin and a firm intention to live the kind of life God says is best. One of Jesus' main characteristics as a Savior, however, is that he is the teacher, above all others, who knows what is a life of deeds pleasing to God; he is unequaled in his knowledge of just what God wants of human beings. As such, Jesus the teacher saves people from a life of foolishness, from a life which, lived in error and darkness, can only end in that death which separates one from the hands of God. To the extent that John's teaching can support that of Jesus, John is a partner of Jesus and not to be separated from him.

2

The Birth of the Savior, His Presentation and Finding in the Temple

From interest in Zechariah's poetic hymn at the naming of John, Luke turns his interest to the birth of Jesus in Bethlehem: a revelation in itself that Jesus is the fulfillment of the David born in Bethlehem. Born in poverty, the child is quickly announced by the Lord's own angel as the Messiah promised to David and to Israel, as Israel's own Lord. One will look in vain throughout the rest of the Gospel for the moment when Jesus actually reigns as Messiah on the throne of David, as Israel's Lord; one will get closer to that moment as one leaves the Gospel and begins the Acts of the Apostles, however, for it is Jesus' ascension which brings him to sit at the right hand of Yahweh and puts him in position to actually be what the angels now announce him to be.

But the titles which are so popular in Luke's time, Messiah (= Christ) and Lord, are once more to be understood as characterized by the title, Savior. Jesus is to be a saving Messiah, a saving Lord. Not only had Zechariah introduced Jesus in this way, but upcoming words of Simeon and Anna will repeat the saving role of Jesus. Indeed, Luke's works stand out among all the works of the New Testament in their witness to Jesus as Savior; by doing this Luke does not let his reader forget the inestimable gift of Jesus, for without him no one could escape the destructive powers which dominate human existence. Surprisingly it is in the Acts of the Apostles that Jesus' offer of salvation, achieved by "calling on his name," is most widely and efficaciously accepted.

2 In those days a decree went out from Caesar Augustus that all the world should be enrolled. [2]This was the first enrollment, when Quirinius was governor of Syria. [3]And all went to be enrolled, each to his own city. [4]And Joseph also went up from Galilee, from the city of Nazareth, to Judea, to the city of David, which is called Bethlehem, because he was of the house and lineage of David, [5]to be enrolled with Mary, his betrothed, who was with child. [6]And while they were there, the time came for her to be delivered. [7]And she gave birth to her first-born son and wrapped him in swaddling cloths, and laid him in a manger, because there was no place for them in the inn.

8 And in that region there were shepherds out in the field, keeping watch over their flock by night. [9]And an angel of the Lord appeared to them, and the glory of the Lord shone around them, and they were filled with fear. [10]And the angel said to them, "Be not afraid; for behold, I bring you good news of a great joy which will come to all the people; [11]for to you is born this day in the city of David a Savior, who is Christ the Lord. [12]And this will be a sign for you: you will find a babe wrapped in swaddling cloths and lying in a manger." [13]And suddenly there was with the angel a multitude of the heavenly host praising God and saying,

[14]"Glory to God in the highest,
    and on earth peace among men with whom he is
        pleased!"

15 When the angels went away from them into heaven, the shepherds said to one another, "Let us go over to Bethlehem and see this thing that has happened,

which the Lord has made known to us." [16]And they went with haste, and found Mary and Joseph, and the babe lying in a manger. [17]And when they saw it they made known the saying which had been told them concerning this child; [18]and all who heard it wondered at what the shepherds told them. [19]But Mary kept all these things, pondering them in her heart. [20]And the shepherds returned, glorifying and praising God for all they had heard and seen, as it had been told them.

21 And at the end of eight days, when he was circumcised, he was called Jesus, the name given by the angel before he was conceived in the womb.

22 And when the time came for their purification according to the law of Moses, they brought him up to Jerusalem to present him to the Lord [23](as it is written in the law of the Lord, "Every male that opens the womb shall be called holy to the Lord") [24]and to offer a sacrifice according to what is said in the law of the Lord, "a pair of turtledoves, or two young pigeons." [25]Now there was a man in Jerusalem, whose name was Simeon, and this man was righteous and devout, looking for the consolation of Israel, and the Holy Spirit was upon him. [26]And it had been revealed to him by the Holy Spirit that he should not see death before he had seen the Lord's Christ. [27]And inspired by the Spirit he came into the temple; and when the parents brought in the child Jesus, to do for him according to the custom of the law, [28]he took him up in his arms and blessed God and said,

[29]"Lord, now lettest thou thy servant depart in peace,
   according to thy word;
[30]for mine eyes have seen thy salvation
[31]which thou hast prepared in the presence of all peoples,

[32]a light for revelation to the Gentiles,
and for glory to thy people Israel."

33 And his father and his mother marveled at what
was said about him; [34]and Simeon blessed them and said
to Mary his mother,

"Behold, this child is set for the fall and rising of
many in Israel,
and for a sign that is spoken against
[35](and a sword will pierce through your own soul
also),
that thoughts out of many hearts may be
revealed."

36 And there was a prophetess, Anna, the daughter
of Phanuel, of the tribe of Asher; she was of a great age,
having lived with her husband seven years from her
virginity, [37]and as a widow till she was eighty-four. She
did not depart from the temple, worshiping with fasting
and prayer night and day. [38]And coming up at that very
hour she gave thanks to God, and spoke of him to all who
were looking for the redemption of Jerusalem.

39 And when they had performed everything according to the law of the Lord, they returned into Galilee, to their own city, Nazareth. [40]And the child grew and
became strong, filled with wisdom; and the favor of God
was upon him.

41 Now his parents went to Jerusalem every year at
the feast of the Passover. [42]And when he was twelve years
old, they went up according to custom; [43]and when the
feast was ended, as they were returning, the boy Jesus
stayed behind in Jerusalem. His parents did not know it,
[44]but supposing him to be in the company they went a
day's journey, and they sought him among their kinsfolk
and acquaintances; [45]and when they did not find him,
they returned to Jerusalem, seeking him. [46]After three

days they found him in the temple, sitting among the teachers, listening to them and asking them questions; [47]and all who heard him were amazed at his understanding and his answers. [48]And when they saw him they were astonished; and his mother said to him, "Son, why have you treated us so? Behold, your father and I have been looking for you anxiously." [49]And he said to them, "How is it that you sought me? Did you not know that I must be in my Father's house?" [50]And they did not understand the saying which he spoke to them. [51]And he went down with them and came to Nazareth, and was obedient to them; and his mother kept all these things in her heart.

52 And Jesus increased in wisdom and in stature, and in favor with God and man.

As the angels praise God and assure peace to those who respond to the plan of God, Mary ponders all this in her heart. Again, she is the symbol of those who, while not understanding the depths of the mystery in which they are involving themselves, hold fast to God and trust and obey him. Mary's role, as far as the Gospel is concerned, is not a prolonged one; yet, one can only feel companionship with her as she tries to understand and inspiration from her as she never lets go the hand of God.

Forty days after Jesus' birth (and thirty-two days after his circumcision and naming day), Mary and Joseph went to the temple in Jerusalem, to that area which is next to the eastern end of the Holy Place (where the angel appeared to Zechariah). Here Mary was purified, for, though not committing any sin, she did, at the birth of Jesus, excrete waste and blood—for this the law of Moses asked a purification. Here also Jesus was presented to Yahweh, but, as the rite showed, Yahweh did not keep the child, but accepted two turtledoves or pigeons instead. Why this rite of presentation? One recalls that every first-born male that opens the womb is given back to God in recognition that life comes from God and ultimately returns to its Owner and Creator, and also in gratitude that this womb is life-producing and, presumably, will now produce more living beings. In a sense, the giving of the first-born is symbolic of giving all the rest of the beings born from this womb—for all life belongs to the Giver of Life. One also should recall, however, the one special occasion in which God asked for all life of the first-born males; this is the story of Passover and the exodus. On that special night God preserved the first-born males of the Hebrews from death, and ever after, in recognition of this saving action and of God's power over the first-born, women presented their first-born males forty days after birth.

At this rite, Simeon, a symbol of the Old Testament in

that he was waiting patiently for the Promised One, recognizes the person of Jesus and, like the Old Testament to the New, yields his life. Simeon's words are particularly important, for they reinforce the proclamation that Jesus is a Savior, and a Savior in such wise that—Luke mentions it for the first time—he will be both glory for Israel and light by which the Gentiles will find the true God. In these few words of Simeon Luke has revealed his own guiding thought, that Jesus' full story is to be played out both in Israel and throughout the entire Mediterranean world, right up to the time and place of Theophilus. Luke does not leave the offer of salvation to the Gentiles to be announced at some later date, as though it were a decision taken only after Israelites chose to reject Jesus. It was always the plan of God that salvation be offered to the Gentiles; indeed, through Abraham and his offspring were all the nations of the world to be blessed, and Isaiah could suggest in his own vision that Israel itself was to be light for the rest of the world whereby the nations would be enabled and encouraged to find and love their Creator. That certain people will reject Jesus and apparently terminate his offering salvation before he even reaches the Gentiles is really no obstacle to God's saving the nations; rather, his plan makes allowance for this rejection and this death. Thus, Luke is able and willing, from the start of his Gospel, to lay the groundwork for his second volume, in which the offer of salvation is brought to the Gentiles and precisely through the continued call upon the name of that Jesus who had apparently been gotten rid of for good. Through Simeon, then, Luke prepares his reader for the further realization that the plan of salvation will bring Jesus into contact with the Gentiles as their light, as their Savior—if this contact occurs only after Jesus' death and in Luke's second volume, the reader is prepared. It is in support of Simeon's identification of Jesus as the Savior that

Anna, a second representative of faithful Israel, identifies Jesus as the Deliverance of Jerusalem.

Luke adds one more story from the early life of Jesus. According to Mosaic law, Jewish males were to come up to Jerusalem at least three times a year, for the feasts of Passover (our March-April), Pentecost (our May-June) and Booths or Tabernacles (our September-October). In accord with this law, Joseph went to Jerusalem, accompanied by Mary and his Son, for whom this law was soon to become obligatory. Since travel to and from Jerusalem was done, when possible, in crowds, it is not surprising that parents catch up with their children only after the first day's journey. What is presumed to be not surprising at all is where one should go to find Jesus, if he is not to be found in the caravan, but in Jerusalem. It should be easy to find him, for would not a child—this child—be found in his Father's house? This story is Luke's last before he introduces the adult Jesus. As such it reminds the reader, represented by Mary and Joseph, that the angel had identified as the father-element in the creation of Jesus the very Spirit and Power of God himself. All the infancy narrative of Luke has delved into the meaning of Jesus in preparation for the narration of his story. The last image Luke wants to leave with his reader is that of Jesus as Son of God.

A secondary note is struck by Luke in this story of Jesus in the temple; that he astounds the teachers of Israel is a foreshadowing of the special feature of Jesus' saving work: he saves by teaching people how to live life as God wants it lived. In his understanding of God's will Jesus astounds Israel.

Luke concludes this story by a notice of Jesus' growth in wisdom, stature and favor. Luke is a master at short summaries which have the power to cover many years, though the descriptions are brief. The growth of John in the desert

(Lk 1:80) and the growth of Jesus in Nazareth (Lk 2:52) are the images which bridge the years until we meet the dynamic, active, adult John and Jesus as they activate the plan of God to which the reader has been introduced. It has been a plan so described by Luke that one can say it has already been long talked of in the Old Testament: what God said he would do, he is now going to do.

3

The Preaching and Imprisonment of John • The Baptism and Ancestry of Jesus

The very language and style of the first two chapters, and not only the images, reminds one of the Septuagint, the translation into Greek of the Hebrew Scriptures for those Jews, particularly of Alexandria in Egypt, who had lost their knowledge of Hebrew in favor of the modern Greek language. Thus, Luke tries, even through style and vocabulary, to have his reader feel that what is recounted in the first two chapters of the Gospel is blossoming right out of the hopes and expectations written in the Old Testament.

Now, to begin Chapter 3, Luke uses more Septuagintal style as he says, after the fashion of Old Testament description of prophets, that "the word of God came to John son of Zechariah in the wilderness." Yet, not only is this sentence to remind us of the fulfillment of the Old Testament; it also places the coming of John and the entire story of Jesus in a very up-to-date and cosmopolitan modernity: the story of Jesus is no longer simply an event in a limited, uninteresting, tiny, peripheral part of the world, but is fully part of the story of the Roman Empire, symbolized by its leading rulers, Tiberius Caesar, Pontius Pilate, Herod Antipas, Annas and Caiaphas. We can identify the year in the world's calendars: 28 A.D., according to Rome, 27 A.D., according to Syria. Christianity has grown beyond Palestine, to become a reality of the world.

Under divine impetus, John begins his call for that repentance which is expressed in baptism and hopes for for-

3 In the fifteenth year of the reign of Tiberius Caesar, Pontius Pilate being governor of Judea, and Herod being tetrarch of Galilee, and his brother Philip tetrarch of the region of Ituraea and Trachonitis, and Lysanias tetrarch of Abilene, ²in the high-priesthood of Annas and Caiaphas, the word of God came to John the son of Zechariah in the wilderness; ³and he went into all the region about the Jordan, preaching a baptism of repentance for the forgiveness of sins. ⁴As it is written in the book of the words of Isaiah the prophet,

"The voice of one crying in the wilderness:
Prepare the way of the Lord,
make his paths straight.
⁵Every valley shall be filled,
and every mountain and hill shall be brought
low,
and the crooked shall be made straight,
and the rough ways shall be made smooth;
⁶and all flesh shall see the salvation of God."

7 He said therefore to the multitudes that came out to be baptized by him, "You brood of vipers! Who warned you to flee from the wrath to come? ⁸Bear fruits that befit repentance, and do not begin to say to yourselves, 'We have Abraham as our father'; for I tell you, God is able from these stones to raise up children to Abraham. ⁹Even now the axe is laid to the root of the trees; every tree therefore that does not bear good fruit is cut down and thrown into the fire."

10 And the multitudes asked him, "What then shall we do?" ¹¹And he answered them, "He who has two

coats, let him share with him who has none; and he who has food, let him do likewise." [12]Tax collectors also came to be baptized, and said to him, "Teacher, what shall we do?" [13]And he said to them, "Collect no more than is appointed you." [14]Soldiers also asked him, "And we, what shall we do?" And he said to them, "Rob no one by violence or by false accusation, and be content with your wages."

15 As the people were in expectation, and all men questioned in their hearts concerning John, whether perhaps he were the Christ, [16]John answered them all, "I baptize you with water; but he who is mightier than I is coming, the thong of whose sandals I am not worthy to untie; he will baptize you with the Holy Spirit and with fire. [17]His winnowing fork is in his hand, to clear his threshing floor, and to gather the wheat into his granary, but the chaff he will burn with unquenchable fire."

18 So, with many other exhortations, he preached good news to the people. [19]But Herod the tetrarch, who had been reproved by him for Herodias, his brother's wife, and for all the evil things that Herod had done, [20]added this to them all, that he shut up John in prison.

21 Now when all the people were baptized, and when Jesus also had been baptized and was praying, the heaven was opened, [22]and the Holy Spirit descended upon him in bodily form, as a dove, and a voice came from heaven, "Thou art my beloved Son; with thee I am well pleased."

23 Jesus, when he began his ministry, was about thirty years of age, being the son (as was supposed) of Joseph, the son of Heli, [24]the son of Matthat, the son of Levi, the son of Melchi, the son of Jannai, the son of Joseph, [25]the son of Mattathias, the son of Amos, the son of Nahum, the son of Esli, the son of Naggai, [26]the son of

Maath, the son of Mattathias, the son of Semein, the son of Josech, the son of Joda, ²⁷the son of Joanan, the son of Rhesa, the son of Zerubbabel, the son of Shealtiel, the son of Neri, ²⁸the son of Melchi, the son of Addi, the son of Cosam, the son of Elmadam, the son of Er, ²⁹the son of Joshua, the son of Eliezer, the son of Jorim, the son of Matthat, the son of Levi, ³⁰the son of Simeon, the son of Judah, the son of Joseph, the son of Jonam, the son of Eliakim, ³¹the son of Melea, the son of Menna, the son of Mattatha, the son of Nathan, the son of David, ³²the son of Jesse, the son of Obed, the son of Boaz, the son of Sala, the son of Nahshon, ³³the son of Amminadab, the son of Admin, the son of Arni, the son of Hezron, the son of Perez, the son of Judah, ³⁴the son of Jacob, the son of Isaac, the son of Abraham, the son of Terah, the son of Nahor, ³⁵the son of Serug, the son of Reu, the son of Peleg, the son of Eber, the son of Shelah, ³⁶the son of Cainan, the son of Arphaxad, the son of Shem, the son of Noah, the son of Lamech, ³⁷the son of Methuselah, the son of Enoch, the son of Jared, the son of Mahalaleel, the son of Cainan, ³⁸the son of Enos, the son of Seth, the son of Adam, the son of God.

giveness of sins from God. The words of the Old Testament
are cited to help make fuller sense of John's preaching: he
is preparing a way for the Lord—just as the angel had said
of him in the Gospel's first chapter; as subjects customarily,
upon hearing of the coming of their king or lord, would fix
roads and smooth the entry of their master into their town,
so John encourages that spiritual "smoothing of the roads,
the mountains, the valleys," so that God may easily come to
his people. What is of special interest in this quotation from
Isaiah (40:3–5) is its ending in the promise that all mankind
will see the salvation of God. Once again, both salvation as
promised by the Old Testament and a salvation for all peoples are the suggested framework for thinking about John's
and Jesus' activities. It is reserved for the Acts of the Apostles to complete, for all people, what is here begun in the
Jordan district for Jews.

Mark's Gospel, a source for Luke, had presented the
figure of John rather briefly, accentuating that he baptized
in water, but that Jesus would baptize in the Holy Spirit.
Luke kept this brief picture and expanded it, like Matthew,
by giving actual preaching of John which showed how John
motivated the people to repentance (God is almost here!)
and how he pointed to One greater than he. But Luke goes
even further than Matthew by giving concrete advice as to
what a repentant person actually does. It is noteworthy that
John, in this Gospel, underlines those actions of repentance
which promote love of neighbor: justice, fairness, sharing.
As one reads the Gospel and Acts, one is struck by the con-
tinuous call for care and concern for the neighbor. John's
preaching, then, fits in well with the preaching of Jesus.

Within his general call to repentance, John called the
Roman-appointed ruler of Galilee, the upper third of Pal-
estine, to give up a marriage which was illegal according to
Jewish law. Herod Antipas, son of Herod the Great, had dis-

missed his first wife to marry Herodias, his distant relative; and Herodias, to facilitate this, had rid herself of her first husband, Philip. In Luke 3:19–20, Luke notes the end of John's preaching, as he reports the eventual arrest of John over this marital matter. Luke 9:9 acknowledges that Antipas had John beheaded (probably at the fortress-jail of Machaerus, south of Jerusalem and east of the Dead Sea), but Luke does not repeat the vivid story of the party, dance and plot which ends in beheading, as does Mark, his source. In Luke 7, John, from jail, sends messengers to Jesus to ask about Jesus' identity as Messiah; this is the only active incursion Luke allows John to make into the Jesus story, once it begins. John is Jesus' co-worker in God's offer of salvation, but he is an unequal co-worker, distinct as are all others from the unique Jesus.

With John as the one inviting all to prepare worthily for God's coming through repentance, Luke now brings Jesus forward. After giving his own approval to the preparation for God implied in being baptized by John, Jesus remains in prayer and it is in this context of prayer to the Father that two important moments are noted by Luke. First, the Holy Spirit of God hovers over Jesus as an indication that he who was born from the Holy Spirit is now empowered and directed by the same Spirit to begin his offer of salvation to all people; from this moment on, Jesus will act under the driving influence of nothing less than the mighty Spirit of God himself. Second, God identifies Jesus as the One he peculiarly loves. Not only, then, is Jesus born of God, but God publicly points out Jesus as his beloved Son. The term "Son of God" had been applied to many types of entities in the Old Testament literature: to angels, kings, Israelites, Israel itself. In Luke's story, Jesus is singled out by God himself as his Son; it is upon him that God, out of love for him, has given the task of representing God and presenting to all

God's offer of salvation; indeed, it is by calling on Jesus' name that a person will be saved. That this choice of Jesus as his representative means that Jesus must die is no argument that God eventually loses his love for Jesus; the resurrection of Jesus by God proves the opposite.

The mention of "my Son" leads Luke to follow the baptism event with the genealogy of Jesus. Why? Because the genealogy is one more way of showing, albeit subtlely, that Jesus can be traced back directly to God as Father. Unfortunately, the genealogy Luke gives does not coincide with that of Matthew, nor can any explanation be given which satisfactorily resolves the differences between Matthew's account of Jesus' ancestry and Luke's account of it. On the other hand, Matthew is not relating the genealogy for the same purpose as is Luke; Matthew wants to link Jesus with Abraham and David, so that Jesus can be seen to qualify, even genealogically, as inheritor and fulfiller of the promises made to those two patriarchs for Israel and for the entire world, whereas Luke is concerned to show that Jesus is, even genealogically, Son of God. That one or other of them has not successfully pieced together all the ancestors of Jesus or has not identified each of the links to our satisfaction does not severely weaken the purposes for which they include these genealogies in their Gospels.

Jesus is now under the active power of the Spirit. The same Spirit will drive him for a testing in the wilderness associated with the Jordan River—then Jesus will be ready to begin his mission to Israel.

4

Jesus Is Tempted by Satan • Jesus Preaches and Cures in Galilee

Luke's principal source, Mark's Gospel, had offered its readers four witnesses about Jesus before Jesus actually began, as the principal character of the Gospel, to be the catalyst and protagonist of the Gospel. These four Marcan witnesses are found in the first thirteen verses of the Gospel and consist of: Mark's own witness that Jesus is "Christ, the Son of God" (v 1); John the Baptist's witness, introduced by an Old Testament text which in its own way witnesses to the truth of John and Jesus (vv 2–8); the witness of the Spirit and the Father (vv 9–11); the mysterious image of Jesus in the desert for forty days, among the wild beasts, tempted by Satan, protected by the angels (vv 12–13).

These four witnesses, these thirteen verses, are accepted by Luke to serve as his own introduction to the principal figure of his Gospel, the adult Jesus, but with some adjustments. Principal adjustments are: (1) the development of Mark's one-verse confession of Jesus as "Christ, the Son of God" into two entire chapters which argue that Jesus is "Son of David, Lord, Son of God, Savior"; (2) the fuller expression of John the Baptist's preaching; (3) the separation of the divine appearance and pronouncement from the actual moment of Jesus' baptism; (4) a description of the actual tempting of Jesus and his responses. Thus, Luke is holding rather well to the outline his Marcan source has given him. Let us consider the last introductory scene: Jesus in contest with Satan.

SCRIPTURE TEXT

4 And Jesus, full of the Holy Spirit, returned from the Jordan, and was led by the Spirit ²for forty days in the wilderness, tempted by the devil. And he ate nothing in those days; and when they were ended, he was hungry. ³The devil said to him, "If you are the Son of God, command this stone to become bread." ⁴And Jesus answered him, "It is written, 'Man shall not live by bread alone.' " ⁵And the devil took him up, and showed him all the kingdoms of the world in a moment of time, ⁶and said to him, "To you I will give all this authority and their glory; for it has been delivered to me, and I give it to whom I will. ⁷If you, then, will worship me, it shall all be yours." ⁸And Jesus answered him, "It is written,

'You shall worship the Lord your God,
and him only shall you serve.' "

⁹And he took him to Jerusalem, and set him on the pinnacle of the temple, and said to him, "If you are the Son of God, throw yourself down from here; ¹⁰for it is written,

'He will give his angels charge of you, to guard
you,'

11 and

'On their hands they will bear you up,
lest you strike your foot against a stone.' "

¹²And Jesus answered him, "It is said, 'You shall not tempt the Lord your God.' " ¹³And when the devil had ended every temptation, he departed from him until an opportune time.

14 And Jesus returned in the power of the Spirit into Galilee, and a report concerning him went out

through all the surrounding country. [15]And he taught in their synagogues, being glorified by all.

16 And he came to Nazareth, where he had been brought up; and he went to the synagogue, as his custom was, on the sabbath day. And he stood up to read; [17]and there was given to him the book of the prophet Isaiah. He opened the book and found the place where it was written,

[18]"The Spirit of the Lord is upon me,
> because he has anointed me to preach good
> > news to the poor.
> He has sent me to proclaim release to the
> > captives
> and recovering of sight to the blind,
> to set at liberty those who are oppressed,
[19]to proclaim the acceptable year of the Lord."

[20]And he closed the book, and gave it back to the attendant, and sat down; and the eyes of all in the synagogue were fixed on him. [21]And he began to say to them, "Today this scripture has been fulfilled in your hearing." [22]And all spoke well of him, and wondered at the gracious words which proceeded out of his mouth; and they said, "Is not this Joseph's son?" [23]And he said to them, "Doubtless you will quote to me this proverb, 'Physician, heal yourself; what we have heard you did at Capernaum, do here also in your own country.' " [24]And he said, "Truly, I say to you, no prophet is acceptable in his own country. [25]But in truth, I tell you, there were many widows in Israel in the days of Elijah, when the heaven was shut up three years and six months, when there came a great famine over all the land; [26]and Elijah was sent to none of them but only to Zarephath, in the land of Sidon, to a woman who was a widow. [27]And there were many lepers in Israel in the time of the prophet Elisha; and none of

them was cleansed, but only Naaman the Syrian." [28]When they heard this, all in the synagogue were filled with wrath. [29]And they rose up and put him out of the city, and led him to the brow of the hill on which their city was built, that they might throw him down headlong. [30]But passing through the midst of them he went away.

31 And he went down to Capernaum, a city of Galilee. And he was teaching them on the sabbath; [32]and they were astonished at his teaching, for his word was with authority. [33]And in the synagogue there was a man who had the spirit of an unclean demon; and he cried out with a loud voice, [34]"Ah! What have you to do with us, Jesus of Nazareth? Have you come to destroy us? I know who you are, the Holy One of God." [35]But Jesus rebuked him, saying, "Be silent, and come out of him!" And when the demon had thrown him down in the midst, he came out of him, having done him no harm. [36]And they were all amazed and said to one another, "What is this word? For with authority and power he commands the unclean spirits, and they come out." [37]And reports of him went out into every place in the surrounding region.

38 And he arose and left the synagogue, and entered Simon's house. Now Simon's mother-in-law was ill with a high fever, and they besought him for her. [39]And he stood over her and rebuked the fever, and it left her; and immediately she rose and served them.

40 Now when the sun was setting, all those who had any that were sick with various diseases brought them to him; and he laid his hands on every one of them and healed them. [41]And demons also came out of many, crying, "You are the Son of God!" But he rebuked them, and would not allow them to speak, because they knew that he was the Christ.

42 And when it was day he departed and went into

a lonely place. And the people sought him and came to him, and would have kept him from leaving them; [43]but he said to them, "I must preach the good news of the kingdom of God to the other cities also; for I was sent for this purpose." [44]And he was preaching in the synagogues of Judea.

The period of Jesus' temptations, to which Jesus was led by the Holy Spirit which gave him birth and now moves him to begin his mission of Savior—this period is revealed by the three temptations given us by Luke (the same as those given by Matthew, the source of which is "Q"). That two of the three temptations are explicitly introduced as temptations against Jesus as Son of God shows that what is at stake—in the third temptation as well—is Jesus' fidelity to his Father. Will Jesus use his power as a sign that he really does not look for life from God and his word, but looks for it in "bread alone"? Will Jesus, under pressure from the fantastic wonders of the world, worship Satan who dominates it, in the hope that from Satan he will receive a part in this world? Will Jesus accept Satan as his God, in hopes of sharing in Satan's power? Finally, even if Jesus will not worship Satan as the source of all good things, will he at least test his God, to see if his God really will protect him in times of danger? God said that he would protect Jesus—but will he?

In each temptation Jesus lives up to his right to be called Son of God, for he is faithful as a son would be—no matter what the temptation. Jesus looks to his Father's word for life, he worships him alone as God of his life, he needs no proof that God so loves him as to be ready to protect him at any moment. Jesus is truly a Son to his Father. Luke hopes that he has shown Jesus' true allegiance, and hopes that the reader will be inspired by Jesus' example. For his part, Satan ceases—only to look forward to a return when he will put Jesus to the test again, in the Garden of Gethsemane; there we will see how faithful Jesus is at the moment of extreme peril. With the temptations completed Luke has completed his version of an introduction by which the reader should understand better than Jesus' contemporaries who this Galilean preacher and teacher really is. In brief, one is to remember throughout the following narration the truth about Jesus which was revealed in Luke 1:15—4:13. Indeed, with the help of this introduction one will be able to judge the justness of the condemnation of Jesus to death, as well as the preaching of Jesus' followers that he is the Savior of the world.

Mark's opening image of the adult Jesus had been that of one who calls for repentance, for "the kingdom of God is at hand"—and of course one would not enter it if one had not repented and been forgiven his sins by God; Mark then had changed the image to Jesus as teacher about God, God's kingdom, Jesus' identity and right to be heard. Luke, on the other hand, having presented a fiery call for repentance through John the Baptist, presents as the first image of Jesus that of Jesus as teacher. Luke, perhaps unlike Mark, no longer felt that he could motivate people to follow Jesus because the kingdom was at hand; no one knew anymore when the kingdom of God might break into human history. Nonetheless, and indeed all the more, the teaching of Jesus was necessary—to provide a guide to fidelity so that one, now repentant of sin and forgiven, might remain faithful until God, through the Son of Man, does bring his kingdom to earth. Jesus, then, under the power of the same Spirit who brought him into the desert, begins his active life in Luke's Gospel as teacher.

Luke has given practically four chapters to an introduction of Jesus as he appears in the Gospel and in Acts. Now, at the start of that more limited story of Jesus' preaching from Galilee to Jerusalem, Luke provides a story (4:16– 30) which is meant to anticipate in a brief and schematic way the Palestinian career of Jesus. This career is typified by the Old Testament quotation: Jesus has received the Spirit of the Lord, has been anointed (= Messiah, Christ) by the Spirit; thus, certain actions can be expected and interpreted as coming from that Spirit, actions in the main which are proclamation, teaching and preaching, but which may all be summed up in this, that Jesus is presenting to Israel a year in which God assures his people that he will only be forgiving if they will return to and obey him through the words of Jesus. Indeed, what we read from now on in the Gospel is the fulfillment of this prophecy. And indeed, in the Gospel, as in this story, we find an initial enthusiasm and warm reception for the words of Jesus. But then, in the Gospel, as here, murmuring and doubts begin to arise, to such a degree that it becomes evident that, as in Israel's ancient history, God blessed cooperative Gentiles rather than disobedient Israelites, so Jesus would eventually have to turn from his own who reject him to Gentiles who, as Acts shows, accept him. Finally, Jesus is led out to die, as he will be at the end of the Gospel, but, like the ending of the Gospel, Jesus escapes the oblivion to which crucifixion was meant to consign him. Lk 4:16–30 is, then, a brief summary of what we can expect in the rest of the Gospel and an interpretation of it all.

Luke, like Mark, is eager to use the next story, the cure of a possessed man, at the beginning of his Gospel, for the way in which the story is told emphasizes the power of Jesus' word: the story underlines the wonderfulness of a word of curing, but concludes with praise of the words of Jesus' teaching. It is Luke's hope that the reader will believe that the power inherent in the curing word is the power to give life which characterizes the teaching word. For it is through teaching rather than through miracles that the Christian is best led into God's kingdom whenever it comes.

Through the cure of Simon's mother-in-law (Simon had been introduced in Mark before his mother-in-law had been cured) and other cures as well, Jesus has revealed himself as having the power usually associated only with the actual presence of the kingdom; Jesus, therefore, is not just in advance of the kingdom, but in some ways initiating it. But a caution is necessary: to call Jesus the Christ, the bringer of the kingdom, solely because he exercises the power of the kingdom is to set oneself up for a delusion, for part of the very career of the Christ is the powerless and humiliating and painful death he must undergo. If one is not prepared to expect this tragedy as part of the lot of the Messiah, one had best not call Jesus Messiah.

Finally, Jesus notes his own sense of his mission: he must go to the other towns, too, to proclaim what he knows of God's kingdom—all to help people to be ready to enter it.

5

The First Five Disciples Are Called • Miracles of Jesus, and Conflicts

In Mark's Gospel, the first action Jesus takes after announcing that the kingdom of God is at hand is to call four men—Peter and Andrew, James and John—who will eventually help make up the Twelve, the successors in symbol of the Twelve sons of Jacob, upon whom the twelve tribes of Israel, the people of God, were founded. Luke puts off the calling of these four men until after Jesus has worked some miracles and has had the chance to become known and praised. Yet, it is not just Jesus' reputation, nor his singular healing of Simon's mother-in-law, that moved these four to leave all and follow Jesus. Rather, Jesus, within the larger framework of his role as teacher, so astounds Peter (in Luke, it is Peter who is at the center of attention) with the miracle of the fish that Peter is visibly shaken and in awe of Jesus. Peter senses that he is in the presence of divine power and immediately thinks of his unworthiness, his sinfulness. The response of Jesus to Peter's abasement is that Peter will now turn to catching men, not fish. In this fashion Luke has begun the collection of that Twelve upon whom Jesus will build the people of God.

Though Peter is the center of the Lucan story, it is clear by the end that more than he are responsive to follow Jesus; this number definitely includes the brothers, James and John. Is Andrew, Peter's brother, also included here? He is not named; however, there is, in v 7 and v 9, a reference to those who worked in Simon Peter's boat and to "all Peter's

SCRIPTURE TEXT

5 While the people pressed upon him to hear the word of God, he was standing by the lake of Gennesaret. [2]And he saw two boats by the lake; but the fishermen had gone out of them and were washing their nets. [3]Getting into one of the boats, which was Simon's, he asked him to put out a little from the land. And he sat down and taught the people from the boat. [4]And when he had ceased speaking, he said to Simon, "Put out into the deep and let down your nets for a catch." [5]And Simon answered, "Master, we toiled all night and took nothing! But at your word I will let down the nets." [6]And when they had done this, they enclosed a great shoal of fish; and as their nets were breaking, [7]they beckoned to their partners in the other boat to come and help them. And they came and filled both the boats, so that they began to sink. [8]But when Simon Peter saw it, he fell down at Jesus' knees, saying, "Depart from me, for I am a sinful man, O Lord." [9]For he was astonished, and all that were with him, at the catch of fish which they had taken; [10]and so also were James and John, sons of Zebedee, who were partners with Simon. And Jesus said to Simon, "Do not be afraid; henceforth you will be catching men." [11]And when they had brought their boats to land, they left everything and followed him.

12 While he was in one of the cities, there came a man full of leprosy; and when he saw Jesus, he fell on his face and besought him, "Lord, if you will, you can make me clean." [13]And he stretched out his hand, and touched him, saying, "I will; be clean." And immediately the leprosy left him. [14]And he charged him to tell no one; but

"go and show yourself to the priest, and make an offering for your cleansing, as Moses commanded, for a proof to the people." ¹⁵But so much the more the report went abroad concerning him; and great multitudes gathered to hear and to be healed of their infirmities. ¹⁶But he withdrew to the wilderness and prayed.

17 On one of those days, as he was teaching, there were Pharisees and teachers of the law sitting by, who had come from every village of Galilee and Judea and from Jerusalem; and the power of the Lord was with him to heal. ¹⁸And behold, men were bringing on a bed a man who was paralyzed, and they sought to bring him in and lay him before Jesus; ¹⁹but finding no way to bring him in, because of the crowd, they went up on the roof and let him down with his bed through the tiles into the midst before Jesus. ²⁰And when he saw their faith he said, "Man, your sins are forgiven you." ²¹And the scribes and the Pharisees began to question, saying, "Who is this that speaks blasphemies? Who can forgive sins but God only?" ²²When Jesus perceived their questionings, he answered them, "Why do you question in your hearts? ²³Which is easier, to say, 'Your sins are forgiven you,' or to say, 'Rise and walk'? ²⁴But that you may know that the Son of man has authority on earth to forgive sins"—he said to the man who was paralyzed—"I say to you, rise, take up your bed and go home." ²⁵And immediately he rose before them, and took up that on which he lay, and went home, glorifying God. ²⁶And amazement seized them all, and they glorified God and were filled with awe, saying, "We have seen strange things today."

27 After this he went out, and saw a tax collector, named Levi, sitting at the tax office; and he said to him, "Follow me." ²⁸And he left everything, and rose and followed him.

29 And Levi made him a great feast in his house; and there was a large company of tax collectors and others sitting at table with them. [30]And the Pharisees and their scribes murmured against his disciples, saying, "Why do you eat and drink with tax collectors and sinners?" [31]And Jesus answered them, "Those who are well have no need of a physician, but those who are sick; [32]I have not come to call the righteous, but sinners to repentance."

33 And they said to him, "The disciples of John fast often and offer prayers, and so do the disciples of the Pharisees, but yours eat and drink." [34]And Jesus said to them, "Can you make wedding guests fast while the bridegroom is with them? [35]The days will come, when the bridegroom is taken away from them, and then they will fast in those days." [36]He told them a parable also: "No one tears a piece from a new garment and puts it upon an old garment; if he does, he will tear the new, and the piece from the new will not match the old. [37]And no one puts new wine into old wineskins; if he does, the new wine will burst the skins and it will be spilled, and the skins will be destroyed. [38]But new wine must be put into fresh wineskins. [39]And no one after drinking old wine desires new; for he says, 'The old is good.' "

companions." Perhaps it is this group of people who at the
end of the story "bring in their boats, leave everything and
follow Jesus." Certainly, Andrew does appear, without introduction, in the formal list of the Twelve (Lk 6:14–16).

What is important in this Lucan story is the accent put
on the role of Peter who follows Jesus: he is to be a fisher
for human beings. It is reasonable to expect, within a piece
of literature, that such a promise be fulfilled for the reader
who is led to expect its fulfillment. Indeed, there is a moment in which the Twelve do go out on their own to preach
and to cure (Lk 9:1–6.10), but the story is so briefly told
that one wonders if this is truly to be understood as the sum
total of what "fisher of men" really means. It seems better
to see the fulfillment of this fishing image in the preaching
and success of Peter and his companions which Luke narrates in the Acts of the Apostles; such indeed is the unity
between Luke's two volumes.

It is also the pecularity of this Lucan story that the image, "fisher of men" is given explicitly only to Peter; one can
extend this image to those who followed Jesus with Peter,
to those who were chosen as the Twelve in Luke 6. One
cannot, however, miss the accentuation of Peter, no doubt
in anticipation of his role in both the Gospel and Acts, especially when one notes how Mark, Luke's source, described
this call of the "fishers of men."

Luke now follows Mark's geography and chronology,
loosely expressed as they are. Jesus, always willing to cure,
even when not asked, immediately responds to the need of
a leper. But wonderful as the miracle is, Luke turns the reader's attention to the willingness and eagerness of Jesus that
the man go immediately to fulfill the Mosaic law. From the
beginning, then, Jesus is clearly shown as one who abides
by the Mosaic law, contrary to the accusations which will
ultimately lead him to death. Moreover, wonderful as the

miracle is, Jesus flees acclaim, preferring teaching, curing, and then solitude and prayer. Jesus in this way begins to define concretely the kind of Messiah of God he knows himself to be.

Luke next tells the story of Jesus' encounter with the paralyzed man who was let through the roof of the house wherein Jesus was teaching; Jesus has by now built up such a reputation and following that even Pharisees, those fiercely adherent to the Mosaic law, and the scribes, those professionably knowledgeable in the law, gather to see just how this Jesus squares with the religion of Israel. That Jesus, in the face of an obvious request for a cure, chooses to forgive the lame man's sins is meant to be symbolic of that depth of power which physical cure only partially reveals; Jesus is meant to bring about the deepest healing—one can enter the kingdom physically lame, but never if one is not forgiven one's sins. Jesus will not actually do much forgiving in his life in Galilee, but it is clear that it is this power which one should hope he will exercise most surely for one's greatest chance of happiness.

The religious leaders of Israel see in Jesus' offer of forgiveness a blasphemy: in their understanding of Yahweh, only Yahweh has the power to forgive sins. Their claim against Jesus only heightens the point of Luke that it is in Jesus, it is in calling on his name, that human beings will, according to the plan of Yahweh, enjoy the results of the divine power to forgive sins. In brief, Jesus has this power, and his exercise of it here is the best gift he can give for the happiness of the paralyzed man. It is greatly significant that Jesus uses this power without even being asked; it is freely given, and, if one asks why Jesus gives forgiveness, one can only assume it is out of love that he spontaneously forgives.

With the crowd in awe, Jesus leaves, only to encounter

the kind of person who in Israel was so despised and mis-
trusted that he could never be a witness in a trial: a tax
collector, whose name is Levi (or, according to the list of
the Twelve, Matthew). Capernaum was situated on the eastern border of Israel, just at the northern shore of the Sea
of Galilee and at a point where most travelers would cross
from the east into Israel. Suffice it to say, that Matthew or
Levi was authorized to collect a toll from everyone who
entered Israel past him, and that he would make his living
from the just and unjust tolls he was able to get away with.
To this man was given the abrupt command, "Follow me!"
Psychologically, the reader is not well prepared for this command and its obedience; one is asked to remember that Jesus
is Lord and that the proper response to his command, from
any kind of human being, should be total and immediate
obedience. In this way of thinking the story makes sense

The call of Levi/Matthew is meant to give way to a confrontation which both prepares for the eventual desire to
put Jesus out of the way (unjustly, as the evidence and logic
of Jesus' explanations attest) and indicates how Jesus (and
subsequent Christianity) distinguishes itself from the Judaism of the Pharisees and their scribes (again, justly, as Jesus'
replies show).

Pharisees had come to the conclusion that the way to
deal with sinners was to segregate themselves from them,
"to hate them as God's enemies." Jesus takes the aggravating
tactic by which he associates with sinners, an act of love by
which he calls them to repentance. Jesus' method is perceived as a conscious affront to traditional Judaism.

Again, Jesus' disciples are not fasting and praying as traditional, proven masters of the Jewish religion teach their
disciples. The answer Jesus gives goes behind such prayer
and fasting to ask the reason for this type of prayer and
fasting. The traditional reason was that through prayer and

fasting one would hasten the arrival of the Messiah and prepare oneself for entry into the kingdom he would bring. To
pray and to fast, in this sense, suggested that the Messiah
was still to come. On the contrary, Jesus argues, the Messiah,
the Bridegroom, is here—thus, the prayer and fasting which
prepared for him is obsolete, only to be taken up again when
the Messiah is absent until his final coming as Son of Man,
at a time determined by the Father.

It is becoming clear that the mind of Jesus and the mind
of the Pharisees and of their scribes are incompatible; there
is no mixing of them. One either looks at reality in Jesus'
way or according to the ways of the past. Old and new wines
do not mix; they destroy each other. It is also true, in the
way Luke uses this metaphor, that the old does not really
enjoy or want the new; those who were accustomed to the
old wine really do not want the new. In this imagery of old
and new wine is hidden one explanation of why Jesus, for
all the good that he did and for all the reasonableness of his
actions, was not accepted as a representative of the Yahweh
Judaism served.

6

Further Confrontation • Jesus Chooses the Twelve and Gives a Sermon on the Plain

That Jesus did not observe what had become the acceptable interpretation of how God wanted his sabbath to be observed proved a particular source of antagonism, which was the worse because Jesus and his disciples had six other days in which to do what they chose to do on the sabbath. This does not mean, of course, that Jesus intentionally chose to do things on the sabbath in order to goad the Jewish authorities and publicly spurn the Mosaic law; rather he acted as the need arose.

It is against the sabbath order commanding rest if one engages in work, for clearly to work is to distract the mind and affection which should, on this day, be centered on God. Over the centuries Israelites had come to identify many activities as "work" which takes one away from God. One of these works is harvesting grain, particularly laboring to separate grain from chaff, even if only by a handful, that the Pharisees find the disciples of Jesus engaged in as they walk through the corn fields. The accusation of wrong-doing gives rise to two types of reply, the second of which is monumental in its claim. First, Jesus takes David and his disobedience of a law of Moses in order to get food, as an argument that the law is subject to greater needs: God allows hunger to be sated, even if it means "work" on the sabbath. Second, Jesus claims that, in regard to deciding what is, or is not, allowed on the sabbath, he—the Son of Man—is master of the sabbath. Since then, Christians have never forgotten that

6 On a sabbath, while he was going through the grain-fields, his disciples plucked and ate some heads of grain, rubbing them in their hands. ²But some of the Pharisees said, "Why are you doing what is not lawful to do on the sabbath?" ³And Jesus answered, "Have you not read what David did when he was hungry, he and those who were with him: ⁴how he entered the house of God, and took and ate the bread of the Presence, which it is not lawful for any but the priests to eat, and also gave it to those with him?" ⁵And he said to them, "The Son of man is lord of the sabbath."

6 On another sabbath, when he entered the synagogue and taught, a man was there whose right hand was withered. ⁷And the scribes and the Pharisees watched him, to see whether he would heal on the sabbath, so that they might find an accusation against him. ⁸But he knew their thoughts, and he said to the man who had the withered hand, "Come and stand here." And he rose and stood there. ⁹And Jesus said to them, "I ask you, is it lawful on the sabbath to do good or to do harm, to save life or to destroy it?" ¹⁰And he looked around on them all, and said to him, "Stretch out your hand." And he did so, and his hand was restored. ¹¹But they were filled with fury and discussed with one another what they might do to Jesus.

12 In these days he went out to the mountain to pray; and all night he continued in prayer to God. ¹³And when it was day, he called his disciples, and chose from them twelve, whom he named apostles; ¹⁴Simon, whom he named Peter, and Andrew his brother, and James and

John, and Philip, and Bartholomew, [15]and Matthew, and
Thomas, and James the son of Alphaeus, and Simon who
was called the Zealot, [16]and Judas the son of James, and
Judas Iscariot, who became a traitor.

17 And he came down with them and stood on a
level place, with a great crowd of his disciples and a great
multitude of people from all Judea and Jerusalem and the
seacoast of Tyre and Sidon, who came to hear him and
to be healed of their diseases; [18]and those who were
troubled with unclean spirits were cured. [19]And all the
crowd sought to touch him, for power came forth from
him and healed them all.

20 And he lifted up his eyes on his disciples, and
said:

"Blessed are you poor, for yours is the kingdom of
God.

21 "Blessed are you that hunger now, for you shall
be satisfied.

"Blessed are you that weep now, for you shall laugh.

22 "Blessed are you when men hate you, and when
they exclude you and revile you, and cast out your name
as evil, on account of the Son of man! [23]Rejoice in that
day, and leap for joy, for behold, your reward is great in
heaven; for so their fathers did to the prophets.

24 "But woe to you that are rich, for you have
received your consolation.

25 "Woe to you that are full now, for you shall
hunger.

"Woe to you that laugh now, for you shall mourn
and weep.

26 "Woe to you, when all men speak well of you, for
so their fathers did to the false prophets.

27 "But I say to you that hear, Love your enemies,
do good to those who hate you, [28]bless those who curse

you, pray for those who abuse you. [29]To him who strikes you on the cheek, offer the other also; and from him who takes away your coat do not withhold even your shirt. [30]Give to every one who begs from you; and of him who takes away your goods do not ask them again. [31]And as you wish that men would do to you, do so to them.

32 "If you love those who love you, what credit is that to you? For even sinners love those who love them. [33]And if you do good to those who do good to you, what credit is that to you? For even sinners do the same. [34]And if you lend to those from whom you hope to receive, what credit is that to you? Even sinners lend to sinners, to receive as much again. [35]But love your enemies, and do good, and lend, expecting nothing in return; and your reward will be great, and you will be sons of the Most High; for he is kind to the ungrateful and the selfish. [36]Be merciful, even as your Father is merciful.

37 "Judge not, and you will not be judged; condemn not, and you will not be condemned; forgive, and you will be forgiven; [38]give, and it will be given to you; good measure, pressed down, shaken together, running over, will be put into your lap. For the measure you give will be the measure you get back."

39 He also told them a parable: "Can a blind man lead a blind man? Will they not both fall into a pit? [40]A disciple is not above his teacher, but every one when he is fully taught will be like his teacher. [41]Why do you see the speck that is in your brother's eye, but do not notice the log that is in your own eye? [42]Or how can you say to your brother, 'Brother, let me take out the speck that is in your eye,' when you yourself do not see the log that is in your own eye? You hypocrite, first take the log out of your own eye, and then you will see clearly to take out the speck that is in your brother's eye.

43 "For no good tree bears bad fruit, nor again does a bad tree bear good fruit; [44]for each tree is known by its own fruit. For figs are not gathered from thorns, nor are grapes picked from a bramble bush. [45]The good man out of the good treasure of his heart produces good, and the evil man out of his evil treasure produces evil; for out of the abundance of the heart his mouth speaks.

46 "Why do you call me 'Lord, Lord,' and not do what I tell you? [47]Every one who comes to me and hears my words and does them, I will show you what he is like: [48]he is like a man building a house, who dug deep, and laid the foundation upon rock; and when a flood arose, the stream broke against that house, and could not shake it, because it had been well built. [49]But he who hears and does not do them is like a man who built a house on the ground without a foundation; against which the stream broke, and immediately it fell, and the ruin of that house was great."

Jesus is the surest interpreter of the mind of God in regard to God's sabbath; formerly, it was through the Mosaic law and its traditions that human beings thought they had entry into God's mind.

Another form of work, which was thought unnecessary on the sabbath, was curing. Curing was often a much more difficult and laborious process than that ordinarily described for Jesus in the Gospels. Jesus answers this accusation more than once in the Gospels in more than one way, but here he appeals to the assumption that to give life, rather than to let it be destroyed, is harmonious with the will of the God who has commanded rest on the sabbath. In other words, it does not reflect a good understanding of God to say that God would allow death on the sabbath which could be avoided by a saving effort.

There is here, of course, more than just an expression of opinion and counter-opinion. Given even the little the Gospel has thus far reported, it is clear that Jesus is making such claims and such challenges as to who knows and represents best God's saving will, that traditional Jewish leaders must make some hard choices. By this time in Mark's Gospel the decision was already reached: death. The Gospel's response is: Wherein is Jesus wrong? Wherein has he misrepresented God?

Perhaps it is the suggestion that something "must be done about Jesus" that moves Luke to report that now, after an entire night in prayer, Jesus is moved to pick Twelve who will eventually represent him when he has been done away with. These Twelve succeed the twelve sons of Jacob, upon whom the Old people of God was founded; the Twelve are also called "apostles," i.e., "those sent out," for they will be, as Luke 9:1–6.10 shows, the first to be sent to preach what Jesus preached and cure as he did. It is noteworthy that only Peter, James and John, his brother, have particular roles to

play in the Gospel and in Acts; indeed, in Acts John is only
mentioned as the silent companion of Peter on occasion and
James is mentioned only as he is cruelly killed by Herod
Agrippa I, grandson of Herod the Great. Judas Iscariot is,
from the first, mentioned as "the traitor." Unfortunately,
though Matthew and Mark also give lists of the names of the
Twelve, it is only with great difficulty that discrepancies in
these names can be ironed out.

With the Twelve Jesus descends the mountain and begins again to teach and to cure people from within and without Israel. Here Luke inserts a lengthy teaching of Jesus,
probably drawn in the main from the source we have earlier
called "Q." This sermon of Jesus is traditionally paired with
Matthew's Sermon on the Mount, though Matthew's sermon
is three chapters in length and Luke's sermon is but thirty
verses. It is not the lengths of the sermons which must be
noted, however, but rather the essential point on which they
agree: love of neighbor.

The Old Testament has revealed that God loves two
kinds of poor people in this world: he loves and protects
those who have little or nothing of what he has created and
he loves and protects these Israelites, chosen as his own
people, who remain faithful to him despite the tragedies
which have brought the house of Israel to humiliation and
impoverishment and slavery. It is not always easy to identify
which of these two groups of "poor" Jesus consoles or urges
others to help. There is, too, in the Gospel of Luke a certain
respect for the instinctual response: you rich have had it for
a while; now it is only fair that you change roles with the
poor. Though this "gut reaction" to life's greater inequities
is not the principle by which human destinies are finally
decided, it does reflect an initial reaction of God to hasten
to the side of the deprived and give warning to the wealthy,
the full, those who know no mourning or weeping. Ulti-

mately, the beatitudes and curses of Luke's Gospel (those blessed and those cursed) are meant to assure those who are "slotted" in various levels of enjoyment of God's gifts that God will comfort the poor, that his kingdom, the ulti- mate hope of all people, is still open to them, and that one who has much of this world's goods cannot assume that he will continue to possess God's goods in the eternal kingdom to come. The criteria by which one will enjoy happiness in the next, everlasting world will be quite different from those by which one gains happiness in this transitory world.

After offering consolation to the poor and warning to the rich, Jesus urges all to love of neighbor. Though many examples challenge human conceptions of whom one should love, Jesus distinguishes true love of neighbor and arrives at the thoroughness and universality of that love. If one is hoping to be loved as Jesus describes love here, his words are perhaps no revelation; but if one is to give love, surely his words are taking one beyond any human expec- tations. Jesus asks for love of all, not for the "love" which sinners have, who "love" only with the thought that they will be loved back. Jesus asks that a disciple take the Father for his model in being compassionate; if one is used to Yah- weh's reactions to love and hate of neighbor, one knows what one can expect for loving one's neighbor and for hat- ing one's neighbor. Jesus asks for compassion for the neigh- bor, for no wrong judgment, for no condemnation, for pardon for the neighbor—in imitation of the Father.

To follow a blind teaching, an inferior teacher is to re- main blind and inferior; Jesus is neither blind nor an inferior teacher. Too often judgment is crudely hypocritical or the outer result of inner badness. Let a man's words flow from goodness, from the way of life Jesus teaches!

To confess Jesus as Lord is to have committed oneself to live life as Jesus teaches, to belief that his way of living is the noblest way of living. To live his way is to have found reality against which life and happiness will not be deluded; to live otherwise is to assure oneself that one will only possess, in the long run, delusion and ruin. To love is the surest way to build a house that will last forever, to enjoy the fullest blessings of God in the age that will not pass away.

7

Cures, a Call to Faith • Jesus Identifies Himself, Criticizes the Pharisees as He Is Cared for by a Sinful Woman

Luke, like Matthew, presents a story of Jesus' cure of a servant of the centurion living in the area of Capernaum. Luke's characters in this story underline the good nature and cooperation of this pagan with Jewish interests. Jesus' response is, as always, spontaneously favorable, and eventually the cure of the servant is reported. What takes over center stage in the development of the story, however, is not the cure, or other elements I have just mentioned, but the faith of the pagan in Jesus' ability to save; so impressive is this military man's faith that Jesus is moved to say something the bitter-sweet truth of which rings down through history as praise and complaint: "I have not in Israel found such faith as this." Against the future direction the word of God will take under Luke's pen, away from Jerusalem and to the pagans, this story takes on particular and lasting meaning.

Sometime after the astounding (long-distance) cure of the centurion's servant, Jesus happened to be entering the town of Naim, when he met a funeral cortege coming out of the city. Though the story is told in brief detail, it is clear that emphasis lay on the absolute desolation of the poor woman following the casket: widowed and childless. At this sight, Jesus again responds spontaneously, letting his power express the depths of his pity. He raises the boy from death and gives him back to his mother; not the least of which benefits to this woman will be that she will have a strong

7After he had ended all his sayings in the hearing of the people he entered Capernaum. [2]Now a centurion had a slave who was dear to him, who was sick and at the point of death. [3]When he heard of Jesus, he sent to him elders of the Jews, asking him to come and heal his slave. [4]And when they came to Jesus, they besought him earnestly, saying, "He is worthy to have you do this for him, [5]for he loves our nation, and he built us our synagogue." [6]And Jesus went with them. When he was not far from the house, the centurion sent friends to him, saying to him, "Lord, do not trouble yourself, for I am not worthy to have you come under my roof; [7]therefore I did not presume to come to you. But say the word, and let my servant be healed. [8]For I am a man set under authority, with soldiers under me: and I say to one, 'Go,' and he goes; and to another, 'Come,' and he comes; and to my slave, 'Do this,' and he does it." [9]When Jesus heard this he marveled at him, and turned and said to the multitude that followed him, "I tell you, not even in Israel have I found such faith." [10]And when those who had been sent returned to the house, they found the slave well.

11 Soon afterward he went to a city called Nain, and his disciples and a great crowd went with him. [12]As he drew near to the gate of the city, behold, a man who had died was being carried out, the only son of his mother, and she was a widow; and a large crowd from the city was with her. [13]And when the Lord saw her, he had compassion on her and said to her, "Do not weep." [14]And he came and touched the bier, and the bearers stood still. And he said, "Young man, I say to you, arise."

[15]And the dead man sat up, and began to speak. And he gave him to his mother. [16]Fear seized them all; and they glorified God, saying, "A great prophet has arisen among us!" and "God has visited his people!" [17]And this report concerning him spread through the whole of Judea and all the surrounding country.

18 The disciples of John told him of all these things. [19]And John, calling to him two of his disciples, sent them to the Lord, saying, "Are you he who is to come, or shall we look for another?" [20]And when the men had come to him, they said, "John the Baptist has sent us to you, saying, 'Are you he who is to come, or shall we look for another?' " [21]In that hour he cured many of diseases and plagues and evil spirits, and on many that were blind he bestowed sight. [22]And he answered them, "Go and tell John what you have seen and heard: the blind receive their sight, the lame walk, lepers are cleansed, and the deaf hear, the dead are raised up, the poor have good news preached to them. [23]And blessed is he who takes no offense at me."

24 When the messengers of John had gone, he began to speak to the crowds concerning John: "What did you go out into the wilderness to behold? A reed shaken by the wind? [25]What then did you go out to see? A man clothed in soft clothing? Behold, those who are gorgeously appareled and live in luxury are in kings' courts. [26]What then did you go out to see? A prophet? Yes, I tell you, and more than a prophet. [27]This is he of whom it is written,

'Behold, I send my messenger before thy face,
who shall prepare thy way before thee.'

[28]I tell you, among those born of women none is greater than John; yet he who is least in the kingdom of God is greater than he." [29](When they heard this all the people

and the tax collectors justified God, having been baptized with the baptism of John; [30]but the Pharisees and the lawyers rejected the purpose of God for themselves, not having been baptized by him.)

31 "To what then shall I compare the men of this generation, and what are they like? [32]They are like children sitting in the market place and calling to one another,

'We piped to you, and you did not dance;
we wailed, and you did not weep.'

[33]For John the Baptist has come eating no bread and drinking no wine; and you say, 'He has a demon.' [34]The Son of man has come eating and drinking; and you say, 'Behold, a glutton and a drunkard, a friend of tax collectors and sinners!' [35]Yet wisdom is justified by all her children."

36 One of the Pharisees asked him to eat with him, and he went into the Pharisee's house, and took his place at table. [37]And behold, a woman of the city, who was a sinner, when she learned that he was at table in the Pharisee's house, brought an alabaster flask of ointment, [38]and standing behind him at his feet, weeping, she began to wet his feet with her tears, and wiped them with the hair of her head, and kissed his feet, and anointed them with the ointment. [39]Now when the Pharisee who had invited him saw it, he said to himself, "If this man were a prophet, he would have known who and what sort of woman this is who is touching him, for she is a sinner." [40]And Jesus answering said to him, "Simon, I have something to say to you." And he answered, "What is it, Teacher?" [41]"A certain creditor had two debtors; one owed five hundred denarii, and the other fifty. [42]When they could not pay, he forgave them both. Now which of them will love him more?" [43]Simon answered, "The one, I suppose,

to whom he forgave more." And he said to him, "You have judged rightly." [44]Then turning toward the woman he said to Simon, "Do you see this woman? I entered your house, you gave me no water for my feet, but she has wet my feet with her tears and wiped them with her hair. [45]You gave me no kiss, but from the time I came in she has not ceased to kiss my feet. [46]You did not anoint my head with oil, but she has anointed my feet with ointment. [47]Therefore I tell you, her sins, which are many, are forgiven, for she loved much; but he who is forgiven little, loves little." [48]And he said to her, "Your sins are forgiven." [49]Then those who were at table with him began to say among themselves, "Who is this, who even forgives sins?" [50]And he said to the woman, "Your faith has saved you; go in peace."

arm to support her, rather than be left on the charity rolls of her town and synagogue. The story, however, ends with a further observation, from another point of view, namely, that such sympathetic miracle-working is a sign of God's presence; taught by their history, the people begin to assess Jesus as a prophet through whom God mercifully visits his people.

It is in the light of this raising of the boy from the dead, and of other things Luke has reported about Jesus, that John the Baptist becomes an active part of the Gospel again— even if for only a moment. John, from his imprisonment, asks Jesus if Jesus is "the One who is to come." In brief, Jesus' words and actions strike his contemporaries as the words and actions which characterize, in their estimation, the Messiah of God and the kingdom of God. Is this, then, the introduction of the new age, the passing of the world as human beings, from the time of Adam's fall, have known it?

Jesus' answer affirms that he is the beginning of the kingdom of God, for by him are done and said things which indeed are expressive of a world in which God rules. But there is also the indication that Jesus is not yet to bring about the fullness of that divine kingdom, for he concludes his message to John with the words, "Happy is the man who does not lose faith in me." These words suggest that one must get used to persevering in trusting Jesus, that there is the possibility that one must persevere a long time before the kingdom is fully present.

Luke uses the figure of John not only to set in motion the question of Jesus' identity, but also to begin a critique of those religious authorities who claim unity with God, yet have spurned, first, John and, now, Jesus. John's clothing, conduct and manner of life should convince any honest person that John comes from God. In regard to John, those commonly regarded as sinners and the furthest from God responded to John's preaching by being baptized; those who were thought to be the holiest refused what John called for and thereby, from Jesus' point of view, lost out on what God hoped to give those who would listen to John, God's representative.

Jesus quotes a contemporary ditty which has a number of possible interpretations. Essentially, the ditty speaks of two groups, "we" and "you." The best interpretation seems to be this, that "we," the Pharisees, expected "you," John, to act a certain way if you were from God—and you didn't, so we reject you; "we," the Pharisees, then expected "you," Jesus, to act a certain way if you were from God—and you didn't, so we reject you. The irony within the ditty is that the Pharisees seem to ask a conduct from John which John does not live up to, but which Jesus does live up to—except that, when it comes to Jesus, then the type of conduct the Pharisees will accept is changed, and resembles that which characterizes John rather than Jesus. In short, it looks as though the Pharisees, by changing their demands of Jesus and John, are making sure that they always have an excuse to reject both John and Jesus.

In the light of this criticism of the Pharisees, who do not do even what sinners will do, the story which concludes chapter 7 seems to take on the quality of a parable. That is, though in Jesus' time there was a sinful woman who treated Jesus with the respect he deserved but did not get from a particular Pharisee (Simon) at a particular dinner, the story now deals with the woman as a representative of sinners in general, who responded to John's call for baptism, and the Pharisee as a representative of Pharisees, who generally opposed John and Jesus. The story is particularly well told as it contrasts the actions of a woman who was in her town considered to be a sinner, whether she had been baptized

or not notwithstanding, and the lack of respect and courtesy
displayed by the Pharisee. The story ends with the dinner
guests ascribing to Jesus the power to forgive sins, something we know he can do from an earlier time when he did
forgive the sins of a paralyzed man let down through the
roof to Jesus. There are indications in the story, however,
which suggest that the woman had already been forgiven by
God (as a result of the baptism of John, most likely) and
thus her actions are not actions inspiring divine forgiveness,
but actions expressing gratitude for forgiveness received.
Whether it be Jesus who forgives at this moment, or God
who forgave at an earlier moment, it is clear that Jesus is
justifiably the object of her affection toward God, that it is
he who mediates to her the certitude of her forgiveness,
that it is he who assures her of peace, that it is he who,
again, draws attention to the value of faith in him.

8

Companions of Jesus • His Parables • The Need for Faith • Powerful Cures

Probably the mention of the once sinful, now forgiven woman of chapter 7 suggested to Luke that he draw the attention of the reader to the fact that women, as well as men, accompanied Jesus in his wanderings; some of these women helped support financially both Jesus and the Twelve. Mentioned by name are two women who will have parts to play, by name, at the burial and resurrection of Jesus: Mary from Magdala (a town on the western shore of the Sea of Galilee) and Joanna, whose husband served Herod Antipas, ruler of Galilee. All these women followers of Jesus will see where he is buried, prepare for his proper burial, and be met by those who announce Jesus' resurrection; they, in turn, will tell the disciples of this resurrection. In regard to Mary of Magdala, Luke notes that she had seven demons cast out of her (presumably by Jesus); this demonic possession does not of itself mean she was a sinner—she would have had to do something to qualify for that.

The story of Luke is mature enough now that he can mention two powerful parables of Jesus—and suggest, too, why Jesus spoke in parables. Let us look at the first parable Luke offers us. The first parable Jesus offers is given in light of the fact that large crowds were gathering and people were finding their way to him. The parable has to do with seed which is scattered over various kinds of soil, for the word of God is being spread by Jesus over various kinds of souls; as Jesus tells this parable, he accentuates the fact that,

SCRIPTURE TEXT

8Soon afterward he went on through cities and villages, preaching and bringing the good news of the kingdom of God. And the twelve were with him, ²and also some women who had been healed of evil spirits and infirmities: Mary, called Magdalene, from whom seven demons had gone out, ³and Joanna, the wife of Chuza, Herod's steward, and Susanna, and many others, who provided for them out of their means.

4 And when a great crowd came together and people from town after town came to him, he said in a parable: ⁵"A sower went out to sow his seed; and as he sowed, some fell along the path, and was trodden under foot, and the birds of the air devoured it. ⁶And some fell on the rock; and as it grew up, it withered away, because it had no moisture. ⁷And some fell among thorns; and the thorns grew with it and choked it. ⁸And some fell into good soil and grew, and yielded a hundredfold." As he said this, he called out, "He who has ears to hear, let him hear."

9 And when his disciples asked him what this parable meant, ¹⁰he said, "To you it has been given to know the secrets of the kingdom of God; but for others they are in parables, so that seeing they may not see, and hearing they may not understand. ¹¹Now the parable is this: The seed is the word of God. ¹²The ones along the path are those who have heard; then the devil comes and takes away the word from their hearts, that they may not believe and be saved. ¹³And the ones on the rock are those who, when they hear the word, receive it with joy; but these have no root, they believe for a while and in

time of temptation fall away. [14]And as for what fell among the thorns, they are those who hear, but as they go on their way they are choked by the cares and riches and pleasures of life, and their fruit does not mature. [15]And as for that in the good soil, they are those who, hearing the word, hold it fast in an honest and good heart, and bring forth fruit with patience.

16 "No one after lighting a lamp covers it with a vessel, or puts it under a bed, but puts it on a stand, that those who enter may see the light. [17]For nothing is hid that shall not be made manifest, nor anything secret that shall not be known and come to light. [18]Take heed then how you hear; for to him who has will more be given, and from him who has not, even what he thinks that he has will be taken away."

19 Then his mother and his brothers came to him, but they could not reach him for the crowd. [20]And he was told, "Your mother and your brothers are standing outside, desiring to see you." [21]But he said to them, "My mother and my brothers are those who hear the word of God and do it."

22 One day he got into a boat with his disciples, and he said to them, "Let us go across to the other side of the lake." So they set out, [23]and as they sailed he fell asleep. And a storm of wind came down on the lake, and they were filling with water, and were in danger. [24]And they went and woke him, saying, "Master, Master, we are perishing!" And he awoke and rebuked the wind and the raging waves; and they ceased, and there was a calm. [25]He said to them, "Where is your faith?" And they were afraid, and they marveled, saying to one another, "Who then is this, that he commands even wind and water, and they obey him?"

26 Then they arrived at the country of the Gera-

senes, which is opposite Galilee. ²⁷And as he stepped out on land, there met him a man from the city who had demons; for a long time he had worn no clothes, and he lived not in a house but among the tombs. ²⁸When he saw Jesus, he cried out and fell down before him, and said with a loud voice, "What have you to do with me, Jesus, Son of the Most High God? I beseech you, do not torment me." ²⁹For he had commanded the unclean spirit to come out of the man. (For many a time it had seized him; he was kept under guard, and bound with chains and fetters, but he broke the bonds and was driven by the demon into the desert.) ³⁰Jesus then asked him, "What is your name?" And he said, "Legion"; for many demons had entered him. ³¹And they begged him not to command them to depart into the abyss. ³²Now a large herd of swine was feeding there on the hillside; and they begged him to let them enter these. So he gave them leave. ³³Then the demons came out of the man and entered the swine, and the herd rushed down the steep bank into the lake and were drowned.

34 When the herdsmen saw what had happened, they fled, and told it in the city and in the country. ³⁵Then people went out to see what had happened, and they came to Jesus, and found the man from whom the demons had gone, sitting at the feet of Jesus, clothed and in his right mind; and they were afraid. ³⁶And those who had seen it told them how he who had been possessed with demons was healed. ³⁷Then all the people of the surrounding country of the Gerasenes asked him to depart from them; for they were seized with great fear; so he got into the boat and returned. ³⁸The man from whom the demons had gone begged that he might be with him; but he sent him away, saying, ³⁹"Return to your home, and declare how much God has done for you." And he

went away, proclaiming throughout the whole city how much Jesus had done for him.

40 Now when Jesus returned, the crowd welcomed him, for they were all waiting for him. ⁴¹And there came a man named Jairus, who was a ruler of the synagogue; and falling at Jesus' feet he besought him to come to his house, ⁴²for he had an only daughter, about twelve years of age, and she was dying.

As he went, the people pressed round him. ⁴³And a woman who had had a flow of blood for twelve years and could not be healed by any one, ⁴⁴came up behind him, and touched the fringe of his garment; and immediately her flow of blood ceased. ⁴⁵And Jesus said, "Who was it that touched me?" When all denied it, Peter said, "Master, the multitudes surround you and press upon you!" ⁴⁶But Jesus said, "Some one touched me; for I perceive that power has gone forth from me." ⁴⁷And when the woman saw that she was not hidden, she came trembling, and falling down before him declared in the presence of all the people why she had touched him, and how she had been immediately healed. ⁴⁸And he said to her, "Daughter, your faith has made you well; go in peace."

49 While he was still speaking, a man from the ruler's house came and said, "Your daughter is dead; do not trouble the Teacher any more." ⁵⁰But Jesus on hearing this answered him, "Do not fear; only believe, and she shall be well." ⁵¹And when he came to the house, he permitted no one to enter with him, except Peter and John and James, and the father and mother of the child. ⁵²And all were weeping and bewailing her; but he said, "Do not weep; for she is not dead but sleeping." ⁵³And they laughed at him, knowing that she was dead. ⁵⁴But taking her by the hand he called, saying, "Child, arise." ⁵⁵And her spirit returned, and she got up at once; and he

directed that something should be given her to eat. [56]And her parents were amazed; but he charged them to tell no one what had happened.

though often enough the soil into which he drops the word of the nearness of the kingdom and the repentance and deeds which make one worthy to enter it is not very receptive, there is some soil which surely will receive the word of God and let that word grow to its fullness. The subsequent explanation of the parable, however, stresses the kinds of ways certain soils will not accept or, if they accept, will not let the word of God live and grow. In this explanation of the parable stress is laid on perseverance, once the word of the Lord has been allowed a favorable home.

Between the telling of the parable and its subsequent explanation, the question is raised as to why Jesus teaches in parables. The question may seem out of place, since very often the very purpose of a parable was to make something clear which is not of itself clear at all; yet, it seems that Jesus' parables do not make the kingdom of God any clearer (and thus do not fulfill the ordinary understanding of a parable), and it makes one suspect that his speaking in parables is an intentional obscuring of the subject of the kingdom, instead of an honest effort at clarifying it. Jesus' answer becomes traditional in Gospel narratives. Isaiah had been called to speak to Israel with the assurance that Israel would not listen to him; his preaching, God told him, is to be done precisely so that the stiff-necked and hard-hearted might be guilty all the more for refusing Isaiah's preaching. God knows that Israel will not listen to Isaiah, but he sends Isaiah anyway, precisely so that Israel will deserve even more punishment for its self-inflicted obstinacy. In short, to speak in parables is to speak in a way which surely will lead an already obstinate audience to further blindness, thus assuring greater punishment.

The second parable Jesus uses has as its principal image a lighted lamp. It is the nature of a light to give light, not to be hidden, and to allow nothing to be kept secret or hidden. So it is with the word of God; it cannot not be preached and offered to mankind, nor can it be accepted only with reluctance or partially—it must reach the total person, and if it does not, the little foothold it has will be lost.

It is fitting that, at the conclusion of parables which urge acceptance of the word of God, Jesus defines those who are most loved by him to be those who hear the word of God and keep it.

Luke now picks up three stories from Mark's Gospel which run in succession there. In each of these miracle-stories, the reactions of elements of their audiences are noted, thus underlining the awesome power of Jesus and demanding ever more a revelation of the person who wields it. In the first story, however, there is joined to this awe of the disciples the painful question of Jesus, "Where is your faith?" This simple question is not addressed solely to the Twelve; it is recorded for the benefit of all Christians who will face the deadly waters without benefit of miracle, but only with trust in Jesus as their protection. Indeed, the story in Luke's Gospel can be read to suggest that Jesus' miracle was not necessary, but was done only after the Twelve showed their lack of faith; future Christians should learn to trust Jesus, no matter how high the waves.

The second miracle recounts Jesus' startling control over a legion of devils. Such control surely reveals the divine power in Jesus; there is no other explanation for their total domination. Jesus affirms this as he instructs the released man to tell at home "all that God has done for you."

The final story, involving two miracles which had been associated no doubt even before Mark inherited them, tells of immense power exercised by Jesus; on the one hand, he cures a person "whom no one had been able to cure," and, on the other, he raises from the dead, despite the doubts of many. But once again mingled into these awesome uses of power is the constant refrain: a call to faith in Jesus. In constructing his stories in this way, Luke is not only reporting the majesty of Jesus, but also appealing to his audience to firm up its faith in this majestic and all-powerful Jesus. Eventually, Christians will have to trust, even though there is no miraculous intervention from Jesus; or is he to be followed and obeyed only if he can deliver miracles?

9

The Mission of the Twelve • Multiplication of Loaves and Fish • Peter's Identification of Jesus • Jesus Speaks of His Fate and of Its Meanings for the Disciple • Jesus Is Transfigured and Works a Cure • The Time of the Ascension of Jesus Draws Near

The Twelve are given power and authority over all demons and over all diseases, then are sent out by Jesus to proclaim the kingdom of God; they, like Jesus, go from village to village in their proclamation of what Luke now calls "the good news." This is a putting into action of what Jesus had promised: that they would be fishers of men, but it is only a warm-up for what will be narrated about them in Acts. Presumably in this brief Galilean mission, the Twelve will be housed and fed by those who receive them favorably; Luke knows of a time, however, when the disciples will have to provide for themselves (Lk 22:35–36). The question can be asked, "Do the disciples preach the necessity of belief in Jesus, as they do in Acts?" In the Gospel the Twelve do as Jesus does, and do what he tells them to do, what he empowers them to do. In Acts the disciples' call to belief in Jesus and commitment to him is basically a call to accept what Jesus had preached and to accept the Jesus in whom, as the Gospel shows, certain major and traditional characteristics of the kingdom are being expressed. The emphasis on Jesus in Acts underlines the role of Jesus in the Gospel: it is through him that the kingdom is being realized.

9 And he called the twelve together and gave them power and authority over all demons and to cure diseases, ²and he sent them out to preach the kingdom of God and to heal. ³And he said to them, "Take nothing for your journey, no staff, nor bag, nor bread, nor money; and do not have two tunics. ⁴And whatever house you enter, stay there, and from there depart. ⁵And wherever they do not receive you, when you leave that town shake off the dust from your feet as a testimony against them." ⁶And they departed and went through the villages, preaching the gospel and healing everywhere.

7 Now Herod the tetrarch heard of all that was done, and he was perplexed, because it was said by some that John had been raised from the dead, ⁸by some that Elijah had appeared, and by others that one of the old prophets had risen. ⁹Herod said, "John I beheaded; but who is this about whom I hear such things?" And he sought to see him.

10 On their return the apostles told him what they had done. And he took them and withdrew apart to a city called Bethsaida. ¹¹When the crowds learned it, they followed him; and he welcomed them and spoke to them of the kingdom of God, and cured those who had need of healing. ¹²Now the day began to wear away; and the twelve came and said to him, "Send the crowd away, to go into the villages and country round about, to lodge and get provisions; for we are here in a lonely place." ¹³But he said to them, "You give them something to eat." They said, "We have no more than five loaves and two fish—unless we are to go and buy food for all these

people." [14]For there were about five thousand men. And he said to his disciples, "Make them sit down in companies, about fifty each." [15]And they did so, and made them all sit down. [16]And taking the five loaves and the two fish he looked up to heaven, and blessed and broke them, and gave them to the disciples to set before the crowd. [17]And all ate and were satisfied. And they took up what was left over, twelve baskets of broken pieces.

18 Now it happened that as he was praying alone the disciples were with him; and he asked them, "Who do the people say that I am?" [19]And they answered, "John the Baptist; but others say, Elijah; and others, that one of the old prophets has risen." [20]And he said to them, "But who do you say that I am?" And Peter answered, "The Christ of God." [21]But he charged and commanded them to tell this to no one, [22]saying, "The Son of man must suffer many things, and be rejected by the elders and chief priests and scribes, and be killed, and on the third day be raised."

23 And he said to all, "If any man would come after me, let him deny himself and take up his cross daily and follow me. [24]For whoever would save his life will lose it; and whoever loses his life for my sake, he will save it. [25]For what does it profit a man if he gains the whole world and loses or forfeits himself? [26]For whoever is ashamed of me and of my words, of him will the Son of man be ashamed when he comes in his glory and the glory of the Father and of the holy angels. [27]But I tell you truly, there are some standing here who will not taste death before they see the kingdom of God."

28 Now about eight days after these sayings he took with him Peter and John and James, and went up on the mountain to pray. [29]And as he was praying, the appearance of his countenance was altered, and his raiment

became dazzling white. [30]And behold, two men talked with him, Moses and Elijah, [31]who appeared in glory and spoke of his departure, which he was to accomplish at Jerusalem. [32]Now Peter and those who were with him were heavy with sleep, and when they wakened they saw his glory and the two men who stood with him. [33]And as the men were parting from him, Peter said to Jesus, "Master, it is well that we are here; let us make three booths, one for you and one for Moses and one for Elijah"—not knowing what he said. [34]As he said this, a cloud came and overshadowed them; and they were afraid as they entered the cloud. [35]And a voice came out of the cloud, saying, "This is my Son, my Chosen; listen to him!" [36]And when the voice had spoken, Jesus was found alone. And they kept silence and told no one in those days anything of what they had seen.

37 On the next day, when they had come down from the mountain, a great crowd met him. [38]And behold, a man from the crowd cried, "Teacher, I beg you to look upon my son, for he is my only child; [39]and behold, a spirit seizes him, and he suddenly cries out; it convulses him till he foams, and shatters him, and will hardly leave him. [40]And I begged your disciples to cast it out, but they could not." [41]Jesus answered, "O faithless and perverse generation, how long am I to be with you and bear with you? Bring your son here." [42]While he was coming, the demon tore him and convulsed him. But Jesus rebuked the unclean spirit, and healed the boy, and gave him back to his father. [43]And all were astonished at the majesty of God.

But while they were all marveling at everything he did, he said to his disciples, [44]"Let these words sink into your ears; for the Son of man is to be delivered into the hands of men." [45]But they did not understand this saying, and it was concealed from them, that they should not perceive it; and they were afraid to ask him about this saying.

46 And an argument arose among them as to which of them was the greatest. [47]But when Jesus perceived the thought of their hearts, he took a child and put him by his side, [48]and said to them, "Whoever receives this child in my name receives me, and whoever receives me receives him who sent me; for he who is least among you all is the one who is great."

49 John answered, "Master, we saw a man casting out demons in your name, and we forbade him, because he does not follow with us." [50]But Jesus said to him, "Do not forbid him; for he that is not against you is for you."

51 When the days drew near for him to be received up, he set his face to go to Jerusalem. [52]And he sent messengers ahead of him, who went and entered a village of the Samaritans, to make ready for him; [53]but the people would not receive him, because his face was set toward Jerusalem. [54]And when his disciples James and John saw it, they said, "Lord, do you want us to bid fire come down from heaven and consume them?" [55]But he turned and rebuked them. [56]And they went on to another village.

57 As they were going along the road, a man said to him, "I will follow you wherever you go." [58]And Jesus said to him, "Foxes have holes, and birds of the air have nests; but the Son of man has nowhere to lay his head." [59]To another he said, "Follow me." But he said, "Lord, let me first go and bury my father." [60]But he said to him, "Leave the dead to bury their own dead; but as for you, go and proclaim the kingdom of God." [61]Another said, "I will follow you, Lord; but let me first say farewell to those at my home." [62]Jesus said to him, "No one who puts his

hand to the plow and looks back is fit for the kingdom of God."

Luke now returns to another, constantly developing theme: the identity of Jesus. Here it is Herod Antipas, who by this time in Luke's story-line has done away with John the Baptist, who reflects the puzzlement of so many Jews: Is Jesus John resurrected? Elijah returned (Elijah never really did die)? Some other prophet of old brought back to life? Herod is the central figure of this puzzlement, for from it all grows a desire in him to see Jesus—and Luke will oblige by having Jesus brought before Antipas in his time of dire trial (Lk 23:7–12).

An interesting sidelight of these verses is the facile way in which people are described as suggesting resurrection from the dead for John and ancient prophets. The way Luke phrases this suggests that he is not thinking that Jesus simply has the spirit of John or of the ancient prophets; yet, surely he does not look like John or one of the ancients. It is a curious kind of resurrection Luke speaks of here!

How is one to understand the next episode, the multiplication of the loaves and the fish? The miracle of the loaves might draw its importance from the observation that it leads into Jesus' question: "Who am I?" It is a concrete expression of power which suggests that Jesus is John, Elijah or one of the ancient, powerful prophets (Elijah had made a handful of meal last for over a year; Elisha had made one jar of oil into many jarsful and had made twenty barley loaves feed one hundred men with scraps left over).

No doubt the power expressed in the miracle recalls the heroes of other times, but the miracle, as Luke tells it, suggests a further interpretation. The disciples' return from their representation of Jesus sets the scene. Jesus continues the teaching and work the disciples had just done at Jesus' behest. Now, as they bring concern for the people to Jesus in expectation that he will help them, Jesus makes the astonishing suggestion that the Twelve feed the five thousand

people. The Twelve admit their lack of food at hand, but
are ready to go to search for and buy food. Jesus now takes
over and, in a description recalling the Eucharist, distributes
bread and fish through his disciples. There was more than
enough; the left-overs filled twelve baskets. From these details of the Lucan story one might conclude that Luke is
retelling the miracle of the multiplication in a way that reminds his contemporaries that Jesus even feeds his hearers
through the Twelve and their successors with an unending,
eucharistic bread. Thus, the story is not only one of power,
but of Christian Eucharist and ministerial service.

We now reach the point of major emphasis; others have
indicated their estimate of who this Jesus is, who, up to Luke
9:20, has laid the ground for perception of his identity. Peter
it is who gives the profoundest identification of Jesus, the
Christ of God. Jesus never denies this, but his ordering the
Twelve not to spread this title suggests that there is much
more to Jesus than Messiahship based on wisdom-teaching
and miracle-working. Jesus' immediate remarks about the
death and resurrection of himself, under title of the Son of
Man, are meant to qualify the Messianic title which knows
no suffering and humilation. It is fitting that Jesus switch to
the Son of Man title, for, as Daniel 7:13—27 suggested, the
sovereignty and kingship which God will give the Son of
Man will be given only after the Son of Man has suffered
and been humiliated. (And it is the suffering servant figure
of Isaiah 52—53 which will specify that this suffering and
humiliation will be the suffering and humiliation of an Innocent on behalf of those who, except for the generosity of
the Just One, would suffer these extreme pains deservedly.)

To know this about the Jesus whom one follows is to
know something about oneself as disciple. Some hard things
belong to life itself, but the disciple accepts them and lives
through them as did Jesus before him. Some hard things

come from discipleship, whether it be from those who hate the disciple or from the disciple's own having to change his life's habits in order to follow Jesus truly, but in both cases the disciple will accept the hardships in order to remain a disciple. Surely, even loss of life for Jesus is to gain life; surely, to gain life by giving up discipleship is to lose it. If one denies Jesus, what can one expect Jesus to do?

That Jesus, as Son of Man, will have to identify his friends and his enemies when he comes again in glory makes Luke think of another saying of Jesus: some of his disciples now before him will actually see the kingdom of God. Since the Gospel and Acts know that none of Jesus' contemporaries lived to see the return of the Son of Man, Luke must be referring to some other moment of the kingdom than that associated with the future coming of the Son of Man. Some scholars think that Luke is introducing his readers to the following story of Jesus' transfiguration, which then should be understood as a vision of the kingdom, i.e., of the king who is glorified for a moment. I prefer to think that those who will live to see the kingdom are meant to be those who will see the Christian community rising out of Pentecost, repentance, forgiveness and baptism to live the life of the kingdom, where God's rule is the only rule.

Most interpreters link the wondrous manifestation of the glorious Jesus with the announcement of his imminent betrayal and death; those disciples who must undergo the experience of the latter are given something which should buoy them up through the challenge to their faith and trust. In the same vein, God's command to listen to his beloved Servant is a command to believe the prophecy of passion, death and resurrection and thereby suffer through it. Indeed, Luke makes it clear that the chief representatives of all those through whom God spoke his plan that Jesus die and rise should even now be discussing with Jesus his passing from

Jerusalem to the right hand of God. Acts will even give us concrete Old Testament prophecy which spoke of this.

Attached to this transfiguration is a cure which again draws attention to lack of faith, and which in its own glorious way provokes a second gloomy warning of Jesus' imminent impotency and humiliation, where faith must not be lacking. Luke emphasizes the inability of the disciples to understand or comprehend this kind of Jesus, and so prepares us for their running away at the smell of suffering and their slowness to believe at the signs of resurrection.

The second prediction of suffering is followed by two stories which underline the importance of the name of Jesus whose fate seems to be inglorious. For those who carry it, it is what makes them great. Moreover, the name is so dominant over the worst of powers which enslave human beings that even one who is not a follower of Jesus, but who uses his name, will drive out demons. Such a one is an ally in the fight to free people from demonic slavery, an ally "under my name."

Luke has waited, for the length of two brief teaching stories of Jesus, to start Jesus on the road to the fate he has predicted for himself. As Luke formulated Jesus' decision to go to Jerusalem, it is clear that the reader is to enter upon this new phase of the Jesus story in the spirit of Jesus: he "sets his face like flint," with resoluteness and determination, toward Jerusalem. The reader is also to realize that this decision to go to Jerusalem is timed not only to put Jesus in place for his death, but to put him in Jerusalem for his ascension to the Father. Luke wants the reader to realize and keep in mind, through the rest of the story, the real outcome of the story: Jesus is to sit at the right hand of God. However anyone else interprets the upcoming events, the true interpretation is that they are necessary steps by which Jesus is to reach that sitting at God's right hand from where he will pour out God's Spirit and continue his work as Savior of all mankind. In short, Jesus is walking to Jerusalem, because it is time to walk to his Father's right hand.

It is natural to pass through Samaritan towns to reach Jerusalem, and safe enough if one is an adult among an adult crowd. But knowing that Jesus' journey has Jerusalem as its goal, the Samaritans extend their hatred for Jerusalem to inhospitality to Jesus. Jesus' reply is not to punish the Samaritans; he already reflects his willingness to forgive his enemies who will crucify him.

From now until Luke 18:14 Luke by and large chooses to relate stories, particularly those which contain teaching of Jesus about how the disciple is to live his "way" to the Father, which is not found in Matthew or in Mark. Many have tried to find what principle Luke might have used to organize these stories, but a final decision is still unavailable. There is, however, a certain logic in the way one story seems to flow out of its predecessor, and this scheme I follow.

As Jesus is deprived of house and hospitality in Samaria, Luke takes the opportunity to teach the disciples that to follow Jesus means to follow one who "has no place to rest his head." It also means to be so different from others that preaching the kingdom of God takes precedence over those activities which can, often must, preoccupy those concerned with the things of this passing age. It also means that one must be careful that attachments do not lead to a betrayal of the discipleship one has entered upon.

10

*Seventy-Two Others Appointed by Jesus, to
Prepare for His Passing to Jerusalem •
Enlightenment of the Disciples*

Luke further signals the importance of this moment in
his narration of Jesus' life by noting that Jesus appoints a
further seventy-two disciples; presumably these supple-
mented the Twelve in helping prepare the journey of Jesus
to Jerusalem, but it is easy to see in these newly-appointed
a hint of those to come in the Acts of the Apostles who will
supplement the witnessing of the Twelve. Indeed, these seventy-two are very much like the Twelve, judging from the
way Luke reports the same instructions given to them as to
the Twelve (Lk 9:1–6). Indeed, these seventy-two announce
as part of their message that "the kingdom of God is very
near you." Ordinarily, Luke does not speak of the "nearness"
of the kingdom. Yet, Jesus is about to come to the towns
the seventy-two are preparing, and we have seen how he
embodies and expresses certain of the qualities which characterize the kingdom of God. Here, as in Acts, to hear the
preaching is to be faced with a decision—to accept or reject
Jesus. Such a decision it was that, if one decided on rejection, one is making a worse mistake than those made by the
notorious cities of the past: Sodom, Tyre, Sidon. Why is this?
Because "to reject you is to reject me, and to reject me is
to reject him who sent me"; what is left unsaid is the question: "What shall become of those who reject him who sent
me?" Why is the decision of Chorazin, of Bethsaida, of Capernaum more punishable than that of earlier towns? The an-

10 After this the Lord appointed seventy others, and sent them on ahead of him, two by two, into every town and place where he himself was about to come. [2]And he said to them, "The harvest is plentiful, but the laborers are few; pray therefore the Lord of the harvest to send out laborers into his harvest. [3]Go your way; behold, I send you out as lambs in the midst of wolves. [4]Carry no purse, no bag, no sandals; and salute no one on the road. [5]Whatever house you enter, first say, 'Peace be to this house!' [6]And if a son of peace is there, your peace shall rest upon him; but if not, it shall return to you. [7]And remain in the same house, eating and drinking what they provide, for the laborer deserves his wages; do not go from house to house. [8]Whenever you enter a town and they receive you, eat what is set before you; [9]heal the sick in it and say to them, 'The kingdom of God has come near to you.' [10]But whenever you enter a town and they do not receive you, go into its streets and say, [11]"Even the dust of your town that clings to our feet, we wipe off against you; nevertheless know this, that the kingdom of God has come near.' [12]I tell you, it shall be more tolerable on that day for Sodom than for that town.

13 "Woe to you, Chorazin! woe to you, Bethsaida! for if the mighty works done in you had been done in Tyre and Sidon, they would have repented long ago, sitting in sackcloth and ashes. [14]But it shall be more tolerable in the judgment for Tyre and Sidon than for you. [15]And you, Capernaum, will you be exalted to heaven? You shall be brought down to Hades.

16 "He who hears you hears me, and he who rejects

you rejects me, and he who rejects me rejects him who sent me."

17 The seventy returned with joy, saying, "Lord, even the demons are subject to us in your name!" [18]And he said to them, "I saw Satan fall like lightning from heaven. [19]Behold, I have given you authority to tread upon serpents and scorpions, and over all the power of the enemy; and nothing shall hurt you. [20]Nevertheless do not rejoice in this, that the spirits are subject to you; but rejoice that your names are written in heaven."

21 In that same hour he rejoiced in the Holy Spirit and said, "I thank thee, Father, Lord of heaven and earth, that thou hast hidden these things from the wise and understanding and revealed them to babes; yea, Father, for such was thy gracious will. [22]All things have been delivered to me by my Father; and no one knows who the Son is except the Father, or who the Father is except the Son and any one to whom the Son chooses to reveal him."

23 Then turning to the disciples he said privately, "Blessed are the eyes which see what you see! [24]For I tell you that many prophets and kings desired to see what you see, and did not see it, and to hear what you hear, and did not hear it."

25 And behold, a lawyer stood up to put him to the test, saying, "Teacher, what shall I do to inherit eternal life?" [26]He said to him, "What is written in the law? How do you read?" [27]And he answered, "You shall love the Lord your God with all your heart, and with all your soul, and with all your strength, and with all your mind; and your neighbor as yourself." [28]And he said to him, "You have answered right; do this, and you will live."

29 But he, desiring to justify himself, said to Jesus, "And who is my neighbor?" [30]Jesus replied, "A man was

going down from Jerusalem to Jericho, and he fell among robbers, who stripped him and beat him, and departed, leaving him half dead. [31]Now by chance a priest was going down that road; and when he saw him he passed by on the other side. [32]So likewise a Levite, when he came to the place and saw him, passed by on the other side. [33]But a Samaritan, as he journeyed, came to where he was; and when he saw him, he had compassion, [34]and went to him and bound up his wounds, pouring on oil and wine; then he set him on his own beast and brought him to an inn, and took care of him. [35]And the next day he took out two denarii and gave them to the innkeeper, saying, 'Take care of him; and whatever more you spend, I will repay you when I come back.' [36]Which of these three, do you think, proved neighbor to the man who fell among the robbers?" [37]He said, "The one who showed mercy on him." And Jesus said to him, "Go and do likewise."

38 Now as they went on their way, he entered a village; and a woman named Martha received him into her house. [39]And she had a sister called Mary, who sat at the Lord's feet and listened to his teaching. [40]But Martha was distracted with much serving; and she went to him and said, "Lord, do you not care that my sister has left me to serve alone? Tell her then to help me." [41]But the Lord answered her, "Martha, Martha, you are anxious and troubled about many things; [42]one thing is needful. Mary has chosen the good portion, which shall not be taken away from her."

swer can lie only in the difference between Jesus and such
figures as Elijah, Elisha, Isaiah, Jeremiah—a difference which
the entire Gospel has been at pains to elaborate.

Upon the return of the seventy-two there is great joy,
for they report great success over all demons when Jesus'
name is used. Jesus does not forbid rejoicing over this success (though the semitic way of emphasizing something is
to deny absolutely what tends to be overemphasized), but
wants his disciples to realize what is the source of true joy,
of joy which will never be taken away. Indeed, Jesus' picture
of himself watching Satan fall from the sky supports the domination of the seventy-two through use of his name.

To think of the true joy, however, is to realize further
the grounds for that joy, grounds which antecede one's
name being written in heaven: one has received the knowledge of the reality of things, a knowledge which could only
come from the One who has it and can reveal it. To know
the Father is to have the knowledge of what is truly valuable,
truly good, for it is he who defines it all as good, true, and
worthwhile or as bad, false, and useless. Somehow it happened (and will happen again in the story of Acts) that the
learned and clever end up ignorant and foolish; indeed, only
if one will accept Jesus' understanding of the Father will one
be truly learned and clever. When everything is said and
done, the foolish have become the wise—by accepting Jesus' teaching about the Father. To refuse Jesus is to be ignorant of the grounding of all reality, to be ignorant of the
Father.

To accept Jesus as the revealer of the truth about the
Father is to see and to hear what even the great prophets
and kings of Israel's venerable past did not see and hear,
though they longed to.

But the revelation of the Father is not to remain an
abstraction; Luke wants the reader to know the Father in

concrete ways of acting. Thus, he first has Jesus confirm what way of acting leads to life: it is the way by which one loves God totally, as God had already revealed it in the Old Testament. Secondly, Jesus expands the love of neighbor God asks for, in order to make clear that contemporary definitions of neighbor must be replaced by God's definition of neighbor.

The story of the man left for dead on the road from Jerusalem to Jericho is all the more poignant for the unwillingness of those who serve closest to God to help the poor man. It is the hated Samaritan, who himself has been taught by his own version of history to hate Jews, who is able to put aside his hatred under pressure of mercy and sympathy. The "neighbor," then, is the one who needs my love. For Jesus, for the Father he reveals, that is the only definition of the one I should love as I love myself.

In his continuing journey Jesus visits the sisters Martha and Mary. Since traditions have placed the house of these sisters in Bethany (on the Mount of Olives), later generations have presumed that Jesus had already gotten so close to Jerusalem: but the next chapters of the Gospel indicate that this is not so. The story about the sisters and Jesus' answer to Martha's emphasis on service merited, in Luke's mind, retelling. As elsewhere, so here, Luke cannot underline enough the supreme value of listening to and learning about the Father from Jesus. Jesus came to be listened to, not to be served; he came to give the better part, not to receive. How will Martha be happy if she cannot spend time to see and hear what prophets and kings could not see and hear, though they longed to?

11

Prayer, Beelzebul and Criticism of Pharisees and Scribes

Jesus called attention, in his visit to Martha and Mary, to the need to listen to the word of God. In his own way Jesus attended to his Father; often Luke gives a glimpse of Jesus spending the entire night in prayer with his Father. Thus, though he spent day after day in service like Martha, he knew how to spend many hours in union with his Father. On one occasion of prayer his disciples asked that he teach them to pray; the response is what we now know as the "Our Father." If one compares this version of the "Our Father" with that given in Matthew's Gospel, one will note differences (Mt 6:9–13); yet, the differences can be explained and thereby one can get at the essential prayer as Jesus taught it.

It cannot be stressed too much how familiar Jesus wants his disciples to be with God; "Father" is the term which reveals the profoundly loving way in which God relates to human beings and will be the source of many an attitude of the disciple toward God and his creation. From the experience of human beings, particularly in times earlier than that of Jesus and in religions outside Judaism which try to comprehend God, fear is a much more likely attitude to God—respect and praise, as well—than love; it is this "unlikely" attitude which Jesus teaches.

In typically Jewish fashion, one's first words to God are a hope that his name (which stands for him) be kept holy throughout creation, and not defiled or insulted. Also, it is

11 He was praying in a certain place, and when he ceased, one of his disciples said to him, "Lord, teach us to pray, as John taught his disciples." ²And he said to them, "When you pray, say:

"Father, hallowed be thy name. Thy kingdom come. ³Give us each day our daily bread; ⁴and forgive us our sins, for we ourselves forgive every one who is indebted to us; and lead us not into temptation."

5 And he said to them, "Which of you who has a friend will go to him at midnight and say to him, 'Friend, lend me three loaves; ⁶for a friend of mine has arrived on a journey, and I have nothing to set before him'; ⁷and he will answer from within, 'Do not bother me; the door is now shut, and my children are with me in bed; I cannot get up and give you anything'? ⁸I tell you, though he will not get up and give him anything because he is his friend, yet because of his importunity he will rise and give him whatever he needs. ⁹And I tell you, Ask, and it will be given you; seek, and you will find; knock, and it will be opened to you. ¹⁰For every one who asks receives, and he who seeks finds, and to him who knocks it will be opened. ¹¹What father among you, if his son asks for a fish, will instead of a fish give him a serpent; ¹²or if he asks for an egg, will give him a scorpion? ¹³If you then, who are evil, know how to give good gifts to your children, how much more will the heavenly Father give the Holy Spirit to those who ask him!"

14 Now he was casting out a demon that was dumb; when the demon had gone out, the dumb man spoke, and the people marveled. ¹⁵But some of them said, "He casts

out demons by Beelzebul, the prince of demons"; [16]while others, to test him, sought from him a sign from heaven. [17]But he, knowing their thoughts, said to them, "Every kingdom divided against itself is laid waste, and a divided household falls. [18]And if Satan also is divided against himself, how will his kingdom stand? For you say that I cast out demons by Beelzebul. [19]And if I cast out demons by Beelzebul, by whom do your sons cast them out? Therefore they shall be your judges. [20]But if it is by the finger of God that I cast out demons, then the kingdom of God has come upon you. [21]When a strong man, fully armed, guards his own palace, his goods are in peace; [22]but when one stronger than he assails him and overcomes him, he takes away his armor in which he trusted, and divides his spoil. [23]He who is not with me is against me, and he who does not gather with me scatters.

24 "When the unclean spirit has gone out of a man, he passes through waterless places seeking rest; and finding none he says, 'I will return to my house from which I came.' [25]And when he comes he finds it swept and put in order. [26]Then he goes and brings seven other spirits more evil than himself, and they enter and dwell there; and the last state of that man becomes worse than the first."

27 As he said this, a woman in the crowd raised her voice and said to him, "Blessed is the womb that bore you, and the breasts that you sucked!" [28]But he said, "Blessed rather are those who hear the word of God and keep it!"

29 When the crowds were increasing, he began to say, "This generation is an evil generation; it seeks a sign, but no sign shall be given to it except the sign of Jonah. [30]For as Jonah became a sign to the men of Nineveh, so will the Son of man be to this generation. [31]The queen

of the South will arise at the judgment with the men of this generation and condemn them; for she came from the ends of the earth to hear the wisdom of Solomon, and behold, something greater than Solomon is here. [32]The men of Nineveh will arise at the judgment with this generation and condemn it; for they repented at the preaching of Jonah, and behold, something greater than Jonah is here.

33 "No one after lighting a lamp puts it in a cellar or under a bushel, but on a stand, that those who enter may see the light. [34]Your eye is the lamp of your body; when your eye is sound, your whole body is full of light; but when it is not sound, your body is full of darkness. [35]Therefore be careful lest the light in you be darkness. [36]If then your whole body is full of light, having no part dark, it will be wholly bright, as when a lamp with its rays gives you light."

37 While he was speaking, a Pharisee asked him to dine with him; so he went in and sat at table. [38]The Pharisee was astonished to see that he did not first wash before dinner. [39]And the Lord said to him, "Now you Pharisees cleanse the outside of the cup and of the dish, but inside you are full of extortion and wickedness. [40]You fools! Did not he who made the outside make the inside also? [41]But give for alms those things which are within; and behold, everything is clean for you.

42 "But woe to you Pharisees! for you tithe mint and rue and every herb, and neglect justice and the love of God; these you ought to have done, without neglecting the others. [43]Woe to you Pharisees! for you love the best seat in the synagogues and salutations in the market places. [44]Woe to you! for you are like graves which are not seen, and men walk over them without knowing it."

45 One of the lawyers answered him, "Teacher, in

saying this you reproach us also." [46]And he said, "Woe to you lawyers also! for you load men with burdens hard to bear, and you yourselves do not touch the burdens with one of your fingers. [47]Woe to you! for you build the tombs of the prophets whom your fathers killed. [48]So you are witnesses and consent to the deeds of your fathers; for they killed them, and you build their tombs. [49]Therefore also the Wisdom of God said, 'I will send them prophets and apostles, some of whom they will kill and persecute,' [50]that the blood of all the prophets, shed from the foundation of the world, may be required of this generation, [51]from the blood of Abel to the blood of Zechariah, who perished between the altar and the sanctuary. Yes, I tell you, it shall be required of this generation. [52]Woe to you lawyers! for you have taken away the key of knowledge; you did not enter yourselves, and you hindered those who were entering."

53 As he went away from there, the scribes and the Pharisees began to press him hard, and to provoke him to speak of many things, [54]lying in wait for him, to catch at something he might say.

typical of prayer in Israel during the centuries leading up to
the life of Jesus to ask God to let his kingdom come, to let
his world be ruled only by him.

There follow three prayers for essential things of life;
the very asking for them confesses that it must ultimately
be the loving God, the Father, who can and will give them.
They are our daily food, forgiveness of sins, and saving us
from that final testing by Satan which, in Jewish thought,
even the most just and upright persons will find it difficult
to survive. It is a characteristic of both versions (Matthew
and Luke) that, when one asks forgiveness from God, one
reminds him that one has forgiven others; the logical im-
plication is clear: Could one expect forgiveness without having forgiven others?

Jesus has taught his disciples a prayer; now he teaches
them about the Father to whom the prayer is addressed. One
must be persistent in praying to the Father; he will listen.
One must ask and search and knock, for he expects this. As
a Father, God will respond like a father—indeed, where
other fathers fail in their responsiveness, God will not. Indeed, he will give the ultimate gift, his Holy Spirit—a gift
which shows how fatherly he is to us.

The reference to the Holy Spirit now moves Luke to
bring up a particularly pernicious identification of Jesus
made by people who, willingly or not, attributed his work
to the most evil of sources: he casts out demons because
Satan has given him a share of Satan's power over demons.
Jesus argues strenuously against this logic with his own
logic: Why would Satan ever expel his own demons and
thereby frustrate Satan's own goals and threaten his own
kingdom? But if Jesus is right and Satan (= Beelzebul, or
"Lord of filth") is not the source of Jesus' power over demons, what is that source? It is God, and the fact that Jesus

does drive out demons is to be understood as a partial fulfillment of the hoped-for kingdom of God. Up to the moment
of Jesus, the devil had exercised his power; now a stronger
one has arrived and the devil is being overcome. To interpret
Jesus as coming from Beelzebul is "not to be with me, not
to gather with me": it is to be against Jesus, to scatter what
Jesus has tried to gather together.

There is a teaching, however, which finds its place in
the midst of Jesus' driving out demons. It is simply a
recorded fact that a person may well become possessed a
second time; the kingdom of God, therefore, has not yet
completely replaced the power of Satan: Jesus is always in
this age to be called upon for salvation.

Jesus is not from Satan; his is a divine source and he
labors to call people to hear the word of God and keep it.
Wicked are those who pay no attention to him, who identify
him with Satan, who will not repent. These people insist on
signs to prove Jesus is from God, and what he has done up
to now is not enough—nor will it ever be enough. The one
sign which is intentionally given *them* is that of Jonah, i.e.,
the sign of the one sent by God to call the wicked of Ni-
nevah (capital of the Assyrian Empire in, e.g., the eighth
century B.C.) to repentance. These very Ninevites, and the
Queen of the South as well, will condemn these wicked who
will not accept Jesus, but prefer to see him as rooted in
Satan. Jesus is greater than Solomon, than Jonah, for whom
pagans were so grateful.

These people who refuse to hear the word of God and
condemn Jesus are wholly blind and completely dark. Their
eye, through which the lamp's light reaches their interior,
is unsound. The light of Christ cannot enlighten their inner
selves, because the light is blocked at their very entrance:
they will not make that first move summed up in the words

"to listen favorably, to repent." With such willingness to listen favorably, to repent, there is the opportunity that one's
total self will live only in light, with no trace of darkness.

In line with this developing criticism of those who do
not listen to God's word, Luke introduces a harsh criticism
of some Pharisees, then of some scribes. The Pharisees' goal
in life is complete obedience to the entire Mosaic law and
its traditional, authoritative interpretations. Jesus praises
them for the obedience they do give, but he accuses them
of such sins—extortion, wickedness, injustice, vanity, lack
of love of God—that acts they do perform out of obedience
become insignificant. Contrary to their being temples of holiness, they have become like tombs which make unholy
those who are in contact with them. Scribes fare no better
in Jesus' judgment. Their expertise in knowing the Mosaic
law in its deepest significance should have been a help in
guiding people to obeying the law and in making the obligations of the law as reasonable as God himself thought they
were. But these scribes have not helped people fulfill God's
law, even though they could have—and they do not even
keep the law themselves.

Jesus pronounces words of severe condemnation on
such of his generation as have been unwilling to listen to
God's word. Since Jesus is the fulfillment of all the prophets
and messengers of God, the generation in which Jesus
preaches will either reap the fulfillment for which these
prophets and messengers longed, or reap the punishment
which has been heaped up as they were consistently rejected and now the fulfillment is refused. In short, because
Jesus is the culmination of Israel's history, his generation is
the culmination of the hopes and punishments of the good
deeds and evil deeds of their ancestors.

Luke makes the fury of the attack on Jesus increase after
his condemnatory words; the scribes and Pharisees are now

intent on challenging Jesus' claim to know better than they the mind of God and thus refute his accusations against them. Slowly but surely, the case is building against Jesus. Is it a just one? Luke hopes his Gospel is making the answer clear; in Acts he counts on the reader knowing the right answer coming from the Gospel stories.

12

Teachings of Jesus on Courage, Trust, Perseverance, His Time of Suffering

Thousands, Luke tells us, gather to hear Jesus who has severely criticized religious leaders and who is now the object of Pharisaic and scribal attacks. In this atmosphere Jesus' teaching is affected by the circumstances. He had accused the Pharisees of hypocrisy; now he publicly warns his disciples of it, for nothing will remain hidden, even if it be said in the dark. Forthrightness rather than hypocrisy will put the disciples in difficult positions, as it has Jesus, and will cause fear. But the only one to fear is the one who can, through hypocrisy or some other means of betrayal of God and Jesus, cause the harm which is irreparable. Besides, on the side of courage and honesty is God who values a human being more than all else in creation and will not forget him. One who speaks out on behalf of Jesus before men will enjoy Jesus' speaking out on his behalf before God. To speak against the Holy Spirit of God, however, as in the recent accusation that the power behind Jesus is not God's Spirit but Satan, is unforgivable. As Acts will show, some disciples will be brought before the highest courts; they should know that the Holy Spirit will be teaching them then how to protect themselves. Can Jesus say more to encourage his disciples?

Joined to this advice about the harsh circumstances which might surround some of the disciples is Jesus' advice about concern for possessions, an excess of which Jesus had just attributed to the Pharisees. The story is not aimed

SCRIPTURE TEXT

12 In the meantime, when so many thousands of the multitude had gathered together that they trod upon one another, he began to say to his disciples first, "Beware of the leaven of the Pharisees, which is hypocrisy. ²Nothing is covered up that will not be revealed, or hidden that will not be known. ³Therefore whatever you have said in the dark shall be heard in the light, and what you have whispered in private rooms shall be proclaimed upon the housetops.

4 "I tell you, my friends, do not fear those who kill the body, and after that have no more that they can do. ⁵But I will warn you whom to fear: fear him who, after he has killed, has power to cast into hell; yes, I tell you, fear him! ⁶Are not five sparrows sold for two pennies? And not one of them is forgotten before God. ⁷Why, even the hairs of your head are all numbered. Fear not; you are of more value than many sparrows.

8 "And I tell you, every one who acknowledges me before men, the Son of man also will acknowledge before the angels of God; ⁹but he who denies me before men will be denied before the angels of God. ¹⁰And every one who speaks a word against the Son of man will be forgiven; but he who blasphemes against the Holy Spirit will not be forgiven. ¹¹And when they bring you before the synagogues and the rulers and the authorities, do not be anxious how or what you are to answer or what you are to say; ¹²for the Holy Spirit will teach you in that very hour what you ought to say."

13 One of the multitude said to him, "Teacher, bid my brother divide the inheritance with me." ¹⁴But he said

to him, "Man, who made me a judge or divider over you?" [15]And he said to them, "Take heed, and beware of all covetousness; for a man's life does not consist in the abundance of his possessions." [16]And he told them a parable, saying, "The land of a rich man brought forth plentifully; [17]and he thought to himself, 'What shall I do, for I have nowhere to store my crops?' [18]And he said, 'I will do this: I will pull down my barns, and build larger ones; and there I will store all my grain and my goods. [19]And I will say to my soul, Soul, you have ample goods laid up for many years; take your ease, eat, drink, be merry.' [20]But God said to him, 'Fool! This night your soul is required of you; and the things you have prepared, whose will they be?' [21]So is he who lays up treasure for himself, and is not rich toward God."

22 And he said to his disciples, "Therefore I tell you, do not be anxious about your life, what you shall eat, nor about your body, what you shall put on. [23]For life is more than food, and the body more than clothing. [24]Consider the ravens: they neither sow nor reap, they have neither storehouse nor barn, and yet God feeds them. Of how much more value are you than the birds! [25]And which of you by being anxious can add a cubit to his span of life? [26]If then you are not able to do as small a thing as that, why are you anxious about the rest? [27]Consider the lilies, how they grow; they neither toil nor spin; yet I tell you, even Solomon in all his glory was not arrayed like one of these. [28]But if God so clothes the grass which is alive in the field today and tomorrow is thrown into the oven, how much more will he clothe you, O men of little faith! [29]And do not seek what you are to eat and what you are to drink, nor be of anxious mind. [30]For all the nations of the world seek these things; and your Father knows that

you need them. [31]Instead, seek his kingdom, and these things shall be yours as well.

32 "Fear not, little flock, for it is your Father's good pleasure to give you the kingdom. [33]Sell your possessions, and give alms; provide yourselves with purses that do not grow old, with a treasure in the heavens that does not fail, where no thief approaches and no moth destroys. [34]For where your treasure is, there will your heart be also.

35 "Let your loins be girded and your lamps burning, [36]and be like men who are waiting for their master to come home from the marriage feast, so that they may open to him at once when he comes and knocks. [37]Blessed are those servants whom the master finds awake when he comes; truly, I say to you, he will gird himself and have them sit at table, and he will come and serve them. [38]If he comes in the second watch, or in the third, and finds them so, blessed are those servants! [39]But know this, that if the householder had known at what hour the thief was coming, he would not have left his house to be broken into. [40]You also must be ready; for the Son of man is coming at an unexpected hour."

41 Peter said, "Lord, are you telling this parable for us or for all?" [42]And the Lord said, "Who then is the faithful and wise steward, whom his master will set over his household, to give them their portion of food at the proper time? [43]Blessed is that servant whom his master when he comes will find so doing. [44]Truly, I say to you, he will set him over all his possessions. [45]But if that servant says to himself, 'My master is delayed in coming,' and begins to beat the menservants and the maidservants, and to eat and drink and get drunk, [46]the master of that servant will come on a day when he does not expect him and at an hour he does not know, and will

punish him, and put him with the unfaithful. [47]And that servant who knew his master's will, but did not make ready or act according to his will, shall receive a severe beating. [48]But he who did not know, and did what deserved a beating, shall receive a light beating. Every one to whom much is given, of him will much be required; and of him to whom men commit much they will demand the more.

49 "I came to cast fire upon the earth; and would that it were already kindled! [50]I have a baptism to be baptized with; and how I am constrained until it is accomplished! [51]Do you think that I have come to give peace on earth? No, I tell you, but rather division; [52]for henceforth in one house there will be five divided, three against two and two against three; [53]they will be divided, father against son and son against father, mother against daughter and daughter against her mother, mother-in-law against her daughter-in-law and daughter-in-law against her mother-in-law."

54 He also said to the multitudes, "When you see a cloud rising in the west, you say at once, 'A shower is coming'; and so it happens. [55]And when you see the south wind blowing, you say, 'There will be scorching heat'; and it happens. [56]You hypocrites! You know how to interpret the appearance of earth and sky; but why do you not know how to interpret the present time?

57 "And why do you not judge for yourselves what is right? [58]As you go with your accuser before the magistrate, make an effort to settle with him on the way, lest he drag you to the judge, and the judge hand you over to the officer, and the officer put you in prison. [59]I tell you, you will never get out till you have paid the very last copper."

against a person having possessions; it is aimed at that subtle acceptance of possessions as securing one's hold on life rather than acceptance of God as the single most important source of life, under whom all else must find its subordinate and secondary place. Through some process the man in the story relies on his wealth for life more than on God; the wealth that he has made his god, however, does not protect him from the call of the true God to the end of life and to judgment.

Jesus turns from this parable to give reasons, principally from God's own care of nature, why no possession should replace God as the source of life and why, if God is Father, one should have absolute trust in his intention to provide for his child. Jesus is not advocating a naiveté which ignores a human being's cooperation with God in the provision of his daily needs, but he is drawing severely on the meaning of God as Father in a person's life—if he is Father, one must trust his love and live in trust. From such a relationship God will never back off, nor should a disciple look elsewhere for his God and Father. It falls to the All-powerful to love faithfully; it falls to the dependent one to remain faithful and deserving of that love. To suffer want, though remaining faithful, is the great Christian mystery; even it, however, is no convincing argument that God is no longer Father or that one should make something else his god. Jesus' death will argue this forcefully.

Jesus emphasizes the value of good deeds over wealth; the latter will wear out and pass away, but the former last forever—and it is in love of what lasts forever that one's heart rests.

Jesus' remarks have suggested the end of one's life. Luke draws into the discussion, then, remarks of Jesus having to do directly with this moment. Calling attention to the unknowableness of the moment of death in most lives, Jesus can only caution readiness at all moments of life. Even his wisdom cannot overcome death—but it can ultimately out-maneuver it.

When Peter asks if this story of the coming of death and judgment is meant for everyone, Jesus shifts into criteria of a happy judgment: faithful, wise, just, working as he should; the reward will be great, more than he ever thought of. Punishment is also possible, but more painful surely for those who had much given them but still refused to do what the Master asks. There seems an implicit teaching here for Luke's time more than for Jesus' time. It seems to be on Luke's mind, for he spends a long time on the subject in the form of the parable of the talents distributed to three ser-vants by their king, who upon his return from afar asks for talents and their use (Lk 19:11–27).

Jesus' most recent teaching has been in the context of anticipated opposition from religious authorities. This con-text leads him to conclude that indeed his teaching is a setting on fire and that indeed he is to be baptized, im-mersed, in the punishments worked out by his enemies. It is clear to him that the word he must preach is to be, among other things, a cause for deepest division, even among loved ones. The divisions among Jews in the earliest decades of the Church over confession of Jesus bears witness to the truth of Jesus' expectations.

Jesus speaks to the crowds who still are not sure of him or of the rightness or wrongness of his opponents: surely the signs are all about, ready for the reading. Jesus' own words, deeds, way of life, his opponents' words, deeds, way of life, the expectations and prophecies of the Scriptures—are these not all signs by which to read these times (and by which one can predict Jesus' future in Jerusalem)? Jesus urges them to make their decision, to judge for them-selves—else, as the parable goes, they will be soon in a position where they can no longer judge and decide, but will, for lack of choosing him, end up where one cannot ask for another chance at making the right decision.

13

Jesus' Call to Repentance, and Cures on the Sabbath • Parables and Admonishment

Jesus continues to urge his audiences to that repentance which is truly life-saving, even for one's life in this world. One cannot assume, on the other hand, that a loss of life to another means that I am less the sinner; each person knows what criteria to employ to determine his uprightness. In support of his plea for repentance before it is too late, Jesus cites the parable of the man who, under petition of his gardener, is willing to wait two more years to see if his fruitless tree will produce—but after two years?

Benighted, in darkness, is the synagogue leader's condemnation of Jesus' cure of a helpless woman on the sabbath. The leader's logic makes some sense if it were not a human being's suffering at stake; even then, his reasoning would not work in Israel if an ox or donkey needed watering on the sabbath. By the end of the story Luke makes sure that the reader sees how unreasonable the understanding of God's will has become for some Jews, and how the ignorant, common people sense the truth of Jesus' manner and judgment.

Luke adds here two parables about the kingdom, stressing in each instance how small are the beginnings of the rule of God in this world, and yet how thoroughly the kingdom will dominate the world, even in this age. These parables will be fulfilled in the Acts of the Apostles.

Jesus makes his way to Jerusalem. To the question "Will only a few be saved?" Jesus does not give a direct "yes" or

13 There were some present at that very time who told him of the Galileans whose blood Pilate had mingled with their sacrifices. ²And he answered them, "Do you think that these Galileans were worse sinners than all the other Galileans, because they suffered thus? ³I tell you, No; but unless you repent you will all likewise perish. ⁴Or those eighteen upon whom the tower in Siloam fell and killed them, do you think that they were worse offenders than all the others who dwelt in Jerusalem? ⁵I tell you, No; but unless you repent you will all likewise perish."

6 And he told this parable: "A man had a fig tree planted in his vineyard; and he came seeking fruit on it and found none. ⁷And he said to the vinedresser, 'Lo, these three years I have come seeking fruit on this fig tree, and I find none. Cut it down; why should it use up the ground?' ⁸And he answered him, 'Let it alone, sir, this year also, till I dig about it and put on manure. ⁹And if it bears fruit next year, well and good; but if not, you can cut it down.' "

10 Now he was teaching in one of the synagogues on the sabbath. ¹¹And there was a woman who had had a spirit of infirmity for eighteen years; she was bent over and could not fully straighten herself. ¹²And when Jesus saw her, he called her and said to her, "Woman, you are freed from your infirmity." ¹³And he laid his hands upon her, and immediately she was made straight, and she praised God. ¹⁴But the ruler of the synagogue, indignant because Jesus had healed on the sabbath, said to the people, "There are six days on which work ought to be

done; come on those days and be healed, and not on the sabbath day." [15]Then the Lord answered him, "You hypocrites! Does not each of you on the sabbath untie his ox or his ass from the manger, and lead it away to water it? [16]And ought not this woman, a daughter of Abraham whom Satan bound for eighteen years, be loosed from this bond on the sabbath day?" [17]As he said this, all his adversaries were put to shame; and all the people rejoiced at all the glorious things that were done by him.

18 He said therefore, "What is the kingdom of God like? And to what shall I compare it? [19]It is like a grain of mustard seed which a man took and sowed in his garden; and it grew and became a tree, and the birds of the air made nests in its branches."

20 And again he said, "To what shall I compare the kingdom of God? [21]It is like leaven which a woman took and hid in three measures of flour, till it was all leavened."

22 He went on his way through towns and villages, teaching, and journeying toward Jerusalem. [23]And some one said to him, "Lord, will those who are saved be few?" And he said to them, [24]"Strive to enter by the narrow door; for many, I tell you, will seek to enter and will not be able. [25]When once the householder has risen up and shut the door, you will begin to stand outside and to knock at the door, saying, 'Lord, open to us.' He will answer you, 'I do not know where you come from.' [26]Then you will begin to say, 'We ate and drank in your presence, and you taught in our streets.' [27]But he will say, 'I tell you, I do not know where you come from; depart from me, all you workers of iniquity!' [28]Then you will weep and gnash your teeth, when you see Abraham and Isaac and Jacob and all the prophets in the kingdom of God and you yourselves thrust out. [29]And men will come

from east and west, and from north and south, and sit at table in the kingdom of God. [30]And behold, some are last who will be first, and some are first who will be last."

31 At that very hour some Pharisees came, and said to him, "Get away from here, for Herod wants to kill you." [32]And he said to them, "Go and tell that fox, 'Behold, I cast out demons and perform cures today and tomorrow, and the third day I finish my course. [33]Nevertheless I must go on my way today and tomorrow and the day following; for it cannot be that a prophet should perish away from Jerusalem.' [34]O Jerusalem, Jerusalem, killing the prophets and stoning those who are sent to you! How often would I have gathered your children together as a hen gathers her brood under her wings, and you would not! [35]Behold, your house is forsaken. And I tell you, you will not see me until you say, 'Blessed is he who comes in the name of the Lord!' "

"no." The previous two parables had hinted, though, that many birds would find rest in the kingdom, that the kingdom would work its way "through all the dough." Jesus prefers an answer which concentrates on personal effort before it is too late; that he says that many will try and not succeed is a judgment which need not be divine, for he sees all about him the half-hearted, unenlightened way in which people think they are to enter the kingdom, while they refuse him who is the truth and the light. What worries Jesus is not an antecedently predetermined number of saved, but the fact that many do not try hard enough.

Given the make-up of the Christian community in Luke's time, it is not surprising that he ends this warning-before-it-is-too-late with the observation that, sadly enough, it will be Gentiles who will enter the kingdom ahead of the sons of Abraham for whom the kingdom is first opened.

Herod Antipas has desired to see Jesus, but he also desires to kill him; later on, he will be happy to see Jesus and do nothing to save his life. Jesus has no fear of Herod and affirms that he will continue his work in Galilee, though his time of work, he admits, is brief. Not only is it brief, but he is not to continue in Galilee; he is on his way to Jerusalem, according to that age-old necessity that a prophet must die only in Jerusalem.

At the mention of the capital city, Jesus addresses her, expressing his deep regret that he failed to gather her children; he must submit to her characteristic of killing the prophets and messengers of God. Jerusalem has refused Jesus, and so he abandons her. As Luke tells his story, Jesus never does enter Jerusalem, only the temple and its courtyards. In a sense, it is not Jerusalem that kills Jesus, but the leaders of Jerusalem. The only time Jerusalem will see Jesus is at that end of time when Jerusalem will, too late, greet him as the one who comes in the name of Yahweh.

It is a curious twist of the Lucan plan that, while Jesus even at this distance plans not to have anything to do with Jerusalem, he will direct his apostles to begin their offer of salvation in his name in Jerusalem.

14

On a Sabbath, Jesus Cures at a Dinner, Then Teaches the Guests Various Lessons

Still one more time Luke chooses to tell a story in which Jesus cures a very sick person before the eyes of religious officials (here, a "leading Pharisee") on the sabbath, of all days. As before, Jesus cures the man only after he forces the scribes and Pharisees to answer for themselves whether or not the law forbids Jesus to cure such a pitiable man. In the wake of their refusal to answer, Jesus works the cure, but, aware of their stubborn disapproval, sets up a logic which he used with them at an earlier time: if you would not hesitate to pull your child or your ox out of a well on the sabbath, why should I not pull this man out of his sickness, sabbath or not? Clearly, the answer seems to have been: there is greater need in the case of the son or ox to be saved than in the case of this man, but who wants to be responsible for such a judgment as that? Given the various sources of the Gospels which keep coming up with stories of Jesus curing on the sabbath to the anger of Jewish authorities, this sabbath "violation" must have been one of the most serious actions which prodded these authorities to oppose and ultimately get rid of Jesus.

Jesus next takes advantage of his presence at this dinner to argue again against the Pharisees' love of honor among men. The story he tells to convey his point is a good one, but it is doubtful that it is told with the purpose of helping the Pharisees actually get places of honor. Rather, the story

SCRIPTURE TEXT

14 One sabbath when he went to dine at the house of a ruler who belonged to the Pharisees, they were watching him. ²And behold, there was a man before him who had dropsy. ³And Jesus spoke to the lawyers and Pharisees, saying, "Is it lawful to heal on the sabbath, or not?" ⁴But they were silent. Then he took him and healed him, and let him go. ⁵And he said to them, "Which of you, having a son or an ox that has fallen into a well, will not immediately pull him out on a sabbath day?" ⁶And they could not reply to this.

7 Now he told a parable to those who were invited, when he marked how they chose the places of honor, saying to them, ⁸"When you are invited by any one to a marriage feast, do not sit down in a place of honor, lest a more eminent man than you be invited by him; ⁹and he who invited you both will come and say to you, 'Give place to this man,' and then you will begin with shame to take the lowest place. ¹⁰But when you are invited, go and sit in the lowest place, so that when your host comes he may say to you, 'Friend, go up higher'; then you will be honored in the presence of all who sit at table with you. ¹¹For every one who exalts himself will be humbled, and he who humbles himself will be exalted."

12 He said also to the man who had invited him, "When you give a dinner or a banquet, do not invite your friends or your brothers or your kinsmen or rich neighbors, lest they also invite you in return, and you be repaid. ¹³But when you give a feast, invite the poor, the maimed, the lame, the blind, ¹⁴and you will be blessed,

because they cannot repay you. You will be repaid at the resurrection of the just.''

15 When one of those who sat at table with him heard this, he said to him, ''Blessed is he who shall eat bread in the kingdom of God!'' [16]But he said to him, ''A man once gave a great banquet, and invited many; [17]and at the time for the banquet he sent his servant to say to those who had been invited, 'Come; for all is now ready.' [18]But they all alike began to make excuses. The first said to him, 'I have bought a field, and I must go out and see it; I pray you, have me excused.' [19]And another said, 'I have bought five yoke of oxen, and I go to examine them; I pray you, have me excused.' [20]And another said, 'I have married a wife, and therefore I cannot come.' [21]So the servant came and reported this to his master. Then the householder in anger said to his servant, 'Go out quickly to the streets and lanes of the city, and bring in the poor and maimed and blind and lame.' [22]And the servant said, 'Sir, what you commanded has been done, and still there is room.' [23]And the master said to the servant, 'Go out to the highways and hedges, and compel people to come in, that my house may be filled. [24]For I tell you, none of those men who were invited shall taste my banquet.' ''

25 Now great multitudes accompanied him; and he turned and said to them, [26]''If any one comes to me and does not hate his own father and mother and wife and children and brothers and sisters, yes, and even his own life, he cannot be my disciple. [27]Whoever does not bear his own cross and come after me, cannot be my disciple. [28]For which of you, desiring to build a tower, does not first sit down and count the cost, whether he has enough to complete it? [29]Otherwise, when he has laid a foundation, and is not able to finish, all who see it begin to mock him, [30]saying, 'This man began to build, and was not able

to finish.' ³¹Or what king, going to encounter another king in war, will not sit down first and take counsel whether he is able with ten thousand to meet him who comes against him with twenty thousand? ³²And if not, while the other is yet a great way off, he sends an embassy and asks terms of peace. ³³So therefore, whoever of you does not renounce all that he has cannot be my disciple.

34 "Salt is good; but if salt has lost its taste, how shall its saltness be restored? ³⁵It is fit neither for the land nor for the dunghill; men throw it away. He who has ears to hear, let him hear."

aims at riddance of self-exaltation (which is not to be confused with realistic self-appreciation).

Again, against the background of this dinner, Jesus
teaches the kind of love of neighbor he esteems. Give the
dinner, which stands for deeds which express love for all
one's neighbors, to all whom God asks his follower to love.
To Pharisees, who think in terms of reward for good deeds
done, Jesus' teaching should make eminent sense: precisely
because the poor, with whom Jesus wants the Pharisees to
share their love, cannot repay the Pharisees, the Pharisees
will surely have that reward which will be so precious: the
reward from Yahweh himself.

Still at the dinner, Jesus teaches about those God invites
to the banquet. Jews expected to be a central part of the
kingdom of God. Many are the excuses of those who are the
first ones the Master thinks to invite; ironically enough, the
people thought least worthy of invitation will be there—in
place of those who should have been there. This parable
surely reflects the irony of the Acts of the Apostles, where
the entrance of the Gentiles into the people of God is chron-
icled for many chapters.

The dinner is over and its time is past, but Jesus continues his lesson: excuses will not help one enter the kingdom; rather, one will have to be willing to choose
discipleship with Jesus ahead of every other love—even of
one's dear one, one's life, if it comes to that. Such choices
in allegiance to Jesus are so painful that they deserve to be
called one's cross.

With respect to such total dedication to Jesus, Jesus
brings up two examples or parables which have as their
lesson the need for total dedication to Jesus, even if it means
giving up all one has. In each parable, a person is faced with
the need to give his all if his tower or his army is to be a
success; the "cost" one must look to see that he has is the

devotion to Jesus by which he can survive any challenge to his discipleship.

Indeed, this devotion is that which makes all else possible, but which, if it is lost, can find no help in anything else. It is like salt, which gives the taste to everything else, but, if it loses its saltiness, can get it from nothing else. In Jesus' day, salt was acquired in lumps, which then were shaved occasionally to have the crystals which went into soups, etc. If a lump of salt sat around long enough, it lost its saltiness. What would a person do with such a lump? Paths and roads in Galilee were not paved, which proved to be difficult in rainy times. To make such roads walkable, stones or rocks would be put into the roads or paths to give one footing in what otherwise would be muddy footing. Useless lumps of salt would also serve the purpose. It is to this sad condition of the disciple of God and of Jesus who has lost his devotion that Jesus calls his hearers to pay attention.

15

Jesus Welcomes and Eats with Sinners, and Tells Why

Throughout this journey to Jerusalem and to the right hand of his Father, Jesus has in many ways encouraged both religious leaders and sinners to repent and then to live the life they should live before God. Sinners, for various reasons, are willing to listen to Jesus, as they were willing to be baptized by John; whether they were truly repentant or not—some or most, few or all—is not clearly reported, but they continue to listen. The religious leaders have been, for their own part, stung to the quick for their avarice, self-exaltation, injustice, and a lack of love for all their neighbors. This last subject of Jesus' criticism is deeply ingrained in Pharisaic outlook. For one who is absolutely (and rightly) convinced that obedience to God is the essential action of a human being, it is quite possible to look askance and without much love upon those who observe little or nothing of God's law.

In theory, this lack of love for the sinner (which can be called "hatred") is not precisely a personal disaffection; rather, it results from the formula that "he who hates my God will be hated by me"—if the sinner is a great sinner, he will be hated greatly, and if the sinner is less a sinner, he will be hated less. In defense of this attitude, the Pharisee can point out the many times in the history of Israel when God dealt harshly with those who rebuffed him; the Pharisee is doing no more, no less.

After this primary consideration, appeal can be made to

15 Now the tax collectors and sinners were all drawing near to hear him. [2]And the Pharisees and the scribes murmured, saying, "This man receives sinners and eats with them."

3 So he told them this parable: [4]"What man of you, having a hundred sheep, if he has lost one of them, does not leave the ninety-nine in the wilderness, and go after the one which is lost, until he finds it? [5]And when he has found it, he lays it on his shoulders, rejoicing. [6]And when he comes home, he calls together his friends and his neighbors, saying to them, 'Rejoice with me, for I have found my sheep which was lost.' [7]Just so, I tell you, there will be more joy in heaven over one sinner who repents than over ninety-nine righteous persons who need no repentance.

8 "Or what woman, having ten silver coins, if she loses one coin, does not light a lamp and sweep the house and seek diligently until she finds it? [9]And when she has found it, she calls together her friends and neighbors, saying, 'Rejoice with me, for I have found the coin which I had lost.' [10]Just so, I tell you, there is joy before the angels of God over one sinner who repents."

11 And he said, "There was a man who had two sons; [12]and the younger of them said to his father, 'Father, give me the share of property that falls to me.' And he divided his living between them. [13]Not many days later, the younger son gathered all he had and took his journey into a far country, and there he squandered his property in loose living. [14]And when he had spent everything, a great famine arose in that country, and he began to be

in want. [15]So he went and joined himself to one of the citizens of that country, who sent him into his fields to feed swine. [16]And he would gladly have fed on the pods that the swine ate; and no one gave him anything. [17]But when he came to himself he said, 'How many of my father's hired servants have bread enough and to spare, but I perish here with hunger! [18]I will arise and go to my father, and I will say to him, "Father, I have sinned against heaven and before you; [19]I am no longer worthy to be called your son; treat me as one of your hired servants." ' [20]And he arose and came to his father. But while he was yet at a distance, his father saw him and had compassion, and ran and embraced him and kissed him. [21]And the son said to him, 'Father, I have sinned against heaven and before you; I am no longer worthy to be called your son.' [22]But the father said to his servants, 'Bring quickly the best robe, and put it on him; and put a ring on his hand, and shoes on his feet; [23]and bring the fatted calf and kill it, and let us eat and make merry; [24]for this my son was dead, and is alive again; he was lost, and is found.' And they began to make merry.

25 "Now his elder son was in the field; and as he came and drew near to the house, he heard music and dancing. [26]And he called one of the servants and asked what this meant. [27]And he said to him, 'Your brother has come, and your father has killed the fatted calf, because he has received him safe and sound.' [28]But he was angry and refused to go in. His father came out and entreated him, [29]but he answered his father, 'Lo, these many years I have served you, and I never disobeyed your command; yet you never gave me a kid, that I might make merry with my friends. [30]But when this son of yours came, who has devoured your living with harlots, you killed for him the fatted calf!' [31]And he said to him, 'Son, you are always

with me, and all that is mine is yours. [32]It was fitting to make merry and be glad, for this your brother was dead, and is alive; he was lost, and is found.' "

two other kinds of justification for the Pharisee's dissociation from all converse with the sinner: "segregation of the sinner will make the sinner come to his senses and repent," "segregation of the sinner will lessen the influence for evil that he might otherwise have on those trying to be good."

Luke now introduces to his reader three parables which, though Luke probably imagines that tax collectors and sinners hear them, are meant to explain to the religious leaders, Pharisees and scribes, why he associates with sinful people. (The multiple repetition of this complaint against Jesus shows how influential this unhappy association with sinners must have been in the decision to get rid of Jesus.)

What unites the three parables Jesus gives is the constant refrain, "What was lost is now found." Each parable aims at exciting in the reader the joy which one has in finding something that was lost. The key to the lost becoming found is repentance, something which, in the nature of the stories, can only be accentuated in the third parable.

The first parable, of the sheep that was lost but now is found, disconcerts some of Luke's readers, for the finding of the one sheep, indeed the lost one (= the sinner), seems to please God more than the persevering love of those who have obeyed him and never wandered off. Though the parable is capable of being understood this way, I think it is meant to be understood in such a way as to reflect that human experience in which one, at the moment of recovering a precious and lost article, shows a joy and a relief that ordinarily he does not show. That the joy of the return exceeds the satisfaction with what has never been lost is at best only momentary; soon enough the dominant emotion of joy extends to all one's possessions.

The second parable is better understood when the value of a drachma is understood. True, it is worth "only" about fifteen cents in American money, but for these poor people it represented a lot. Consider on the one hand that each Jew's financial obligation for the yearly upkeep of the Jerusalem temple was two drachmas, and, on the other hand, that the country people of today's Egypt spend about two cents a day on food.

Both the first and the second parables have another theme interwoven with that of joy at finding what was lost: the finding is done through the effort of the shepherd, of the woman. The sinner, in other words, will return to God only if Jesus goes after them and associates with them.

Given the direction of thought in the first two parables, the famous and tremendous parable of the prodigal son should emphasize, first of all, the joy at what has been found. The elder son of the parable is a thin disguise for the Pharisees and scribes to whom Jesus is speaking this parable. Given their love for obedience to God, can they not understand the joy at the sinner's return? This parable also deals with a lost object which is human; because of this, circumstances change. Jesus can underline the need for repentance; he can stress the patience of the father, rather than the activity of the shepherd and woman; he can accentuate the significance of what has happened: "This son of mine, your brother, was dead and has come back to life."

Told for the benefit of the Pharisees and scribes and to explain to them Jesus' willingness to associate with sinners and his motivation for this association, the parable must again confront the problem of the joy at the return of a profligate man in contrast to the apparent lack of appreciation of the faithful one. The answer this time is not to be that the joy is only the reaction of this glorious moment, and not a sign of greater appreciation of the repentant sinner. Rather, the answer lies in the reminder that "you are with me always and all I have is yours." Whatever the expressions of joy at the sinner's return (ring meaning sonship

regained, sandals meaning he will not be a slave as he re-
quested, the precious animal as a sign of a joyful banquet),
the sinner has been the loser, for he "was not always with
me and did not share in all I have, for all I had was, for a
very long time, not his at all."

16

Jesus Teaches About Astuteness and Effort to Enter the Kingdom, About the Law of Moses and the Prophets

Over a number of pages of his Gospel, Luke has shown how differently Jesus thinks about values and virtues, about Pharisee and sinner. Through a parable he now accentuates the eagerness and cleverness of people when their well-being and future is at stake in this world; at this moment of anxiety and uncertainty, these people act very cleverly and astutely to safeguard their security. Jesus notes the effort made by these people to save themselves and asks why, in the greatest of all contests for salvation, people are less clever, less eager, less motivated to assure their happiness and security in the age—the eternal age—to come.

The parable, by which Jesus exemplified astuteness in saving oneself from a difficult situation, had to do with money and cheating in order to get more and more of it. Thus, after teaching his main conclusion about cleverness in saving oneself, Jesus makes some comments about money. Will money buy happiness in the next life? No, so in this life use money while you have it to buy friends for the next life. This is tongue-in-cheek teaching which reveals how foolish it is to rely on money for one's happiness.

Jesus draws a number of lessons from the use/misuse of money as seen in this parable: all of them have to do with trusting in greater things the person who cannot be trusted in the use of smaller things. But where does this lack of trust originate? The embezzler, through his stealing, reveals

16He also said to the disciples, "There was a rich man who had a steward, and charges were brought to him that this man was wasting his goods. ²And he called him and said to him, 'What is this that I hear about you? Turn in the account of your stewardship, for you can no longer be steward.' ³And the steward said to himself, 'What shall I do, since my master is taking the stewardship away from me? I am not strong enough to dig, and I am ashamed to beg. ⁴I have decided what to do, so that people may receive me into their houses when I am put out of the stewardship.' ⁵So, summoning his master's debtors one by one, he said to the first, 'How much do you owe my master?' ⁶He said, 'A hundred measures of oil.' And he said to him, 'Take your bill, and sit down quickly and write fifty.' ⁷Then he said to another, 'And how much do you owe?' He said, 'A hundred measures of wheat.' He said to him, 'Take your bill, and write eighty.' ⁸The master commended the dishonest steward for his shrewdness; for the sons of this world are more shrewd in dealing with their own generation than the sons of light. ⁹And I tell you, make friends for yourselves by means of unrighteous mammon, so that when it fails they may receive you into the eternal habitations.

10 "He who is faithful in a very little is faithful also in much; and he who is dishonest in a very little is dishonest also in much. ¹¹If then you have not been faithful in the unrighteous mammon, who will entrust to you the true riches? ¹²And if you have not been faithful in that which is another's who will give you that which is your own? ¹³No servant can serve two masters; for

either he will hate the one and love the other, or he will be devoted to the one and despise the other. You cannot serve God and mammon."

14 The Pharisees, who were lovers of money, heard all this, and they scoffed at him. [15]But he said to them, "You are those who justify yourselves before men, but God knows your hearts; for what is exalted among men is an abomination in the sight of God.

16 "The law and the prophets were until John; since then the good news of the kingdom of God is preached, and every one enters it violently. [17]But it is easier for heaven and earth to pass away, than for one dot of the law to become void.

18 "Every one who divorces his wife and marries another commits adultery, and he who marries a woman divorced from her husband commits adultery.

19 "There was a rich man, who was clothed in purple and fine linen and who feasted sumptuously every day. [20]And at his gate lay a poor man named Lazarus, full of sores, [21]who desired to be fed with what fell from the rich man's table; moreover the dogs came and licked his sores. [22]The poor man died and was carried by the angels to Abraham's bosom. The rich man also died and was buried; [23]and in Hades, being in torment, he lifted up his eyes, and saw Abraham far off and Lazarus in his bosom. [24]And he called out, 'Father Abraham, have mercy upon me, and send Lazarus to dip the end of his finger in water and cool my tongue; for I am in anguish in this flame.' [25]But Abraham said, 'Son, remember that you in your lifetime received your good things, and Lazarus in like manner evil things; but now he is comforted here, and you are in anguish. [26]And besides all this, between us and you a great chasm has been fixed, in order that those who would pass from here to you may not be able, and none

may cross from there to us.' ^{27}And he said, 'Then I beg you, father, to send him to my father's house, ^{28}for I have five brothers, so that he may warn them, lest they also come into this place of torment.' ^{29}But Abraham said, 'They have Moses and the prophets; let them hear them.' ^{30}And he said, 'No, father Abraham; but if some one goes to them from the dead, they will repent.' ^{31}He said to him, 'If they do not hear Moses and the prophets, neither will they be convinced if some one should rise from the dead.' "

the god he truly serves; once one realizes whom the thief serves, he will realize that the thief is not to be trusted with greater responsibilities, because his service of this evil god will make him all the more selfish and thieving. And to suppose that one can serve both the god of money and Yahweh is a pure illusion; history is filled with the story of this unrealistic attempt to live life.

In continuity with what he has presented to his reader, Luke once again brings the Pharisees into conflict with Jesus on the subject of money. It is their love of money, Luke notes, which makes them laugh at Jesus' warnings about involvement with money and especially the service one can find oneself giving to the god of money instead of Yahweh; evidently, the Pharisees thought Jesus' opposition between Yahweh and the god called money was overplayed, or at least in their own case their involvement with money did not lessen their devotion to Yahweh. But Jesus sees it differently; he sees the eagerness of the Pharisees for money to be in fact service of a god other than Yahweh. And this reality is known by Yahweh, though it might be hidden from men who, because they cannot see the real motivation of the Pharisees, praise them as single-minded worshipers of Yahweh alone.

Luke now adds a saying of Jesus which has relevance to the train of thought he has been developing. Up to the time of Jesus and John the religious system characterized by the law and the prophets was dominant; it revealed how human beings were to relate to God. Within this system, Pharisees and scribes had come to be acknowledged as the truest exponents of the fullest relationship to God hoped for in the law and the prophets. Jesus had argued to the contrary: these men are not truly singleminded and singlehearted in their living out the implications of life with God. With John and Jesus has come the preaching of the kingdom

that is the goal for which law and prophets have been trying
to prepare people to enter in worthiness. Knowing the true,
unworthy state of the people, John and Jesus have joined
with their preaching of the kingdom the call for repentance;
only through repentance and the hoped-for forgiveness from
God can people enter into this kingdom. The Pharisees and
scribes cannot see themselves as needing repentance. Jesus,
now as before, indicates that many people, among whom
are those the Pharisees and scribes would condemn as unworthy for the kingdom, are being readied to enter it, for
they do respond to the call to repent. Jesus says that their
entry into the kingdom is "by violence"; in this he is referring back to his parable (Lk 14:23) where the master of the
banquet of the kingdom tells his servants to go out and
"force" people to come in to the banquet, to fill up the
places originally reserved for people who, the master finds,
have more important things to do than eat with him.

To speak this way is not, however, to make little of the
law and the prophets, for through them God spoke his mind
for man's happiness. Though Jesus will adjust the law and
the prophets in order to make them reflect as perfectly as
possible the mind of God, Jesus' followers will recognize that
their morality is rooted in the law and the prophets. One
example, which is cited no doubt because of its need to be
cited in Luke's time, has to do with the sinful aspects of
divorce: the man who divorces and marries another commits a sin against the Mosaic law prohibiting adultery, as
does the man who marries a woman divorced by her husband. Indeed, this one example shows that the law and
prophets are not abandoned by Jesus; rather, one can argue
that he is more demanding than the Mosaic law, for the law
does not consider such examples as Jesus gives to be examples of adultery.

But Luke does not want the discussion to go further

into the law and the prophets; he was interested in speaking about this system of religion because it is the system in which the Pharisees claim to live in virtue, but which Jesus says argues against their claim and supports his own preaching about the kingdom and the need for readiness—repentance—to enter it. Jesus returns to the question of money, or, better, the misuse of it. He gives a parable which has become very famous. It tells of a rich man and a poor man: the two are as close as the rich man's dining room is to his front gate, where the poor man lies in tatters, his festering wounds licked by dogs, and longs for scraps from the rich man's table. That the rich man dressed in purple and fine linen and feasted magnificently every day can only underline the tragedy being played out.

The parable at first seems to allot life in the afterlife solely on the basis that it is only just that the roles of the rich and the poor be reversed; nature itself demands equal opportunity and time for the poor to enjoy wealth and the wealthy to take the place of the poor. It becomes clear, however, that what puts the rich man in Hades or hell is his own lack of charity, his keeping all his wealth for himself while Lazarus is left to die in misery. Why is the poor man in the bosom of Abraham (as the imagery of Luke's day liked to describe the love of God)? Because of virtue? Rather what is accentuated is God's pure sympathy for a person in suffering; it is the same sympathy which moves Jesus to cure, to love—without mention of the person's meriting through virtue.

From the way in which the parable is told, one can understand the justice of the rich man's punishment; with the recording of this punishment the parable seems complete. Yet, the dialogue between the rich man and Abraham continues, and in such a direction that one can see Luke's interest for the generations after Jesus. The rich man no

longer asks for his own betterment; he turns to consider
those who still have the opportunity to repent before they
should enter—and they will enter—the Hades from which
there is no relief or escape. Abraham tells him that his brothers have all the help they need in the guidance offered by
the law and the prophets. The rich man knows the attention
his brothers give to the law and asks that the poor Lazarus
be sent from the grave to them: then they would listen. The
answer is ominous, both for Jesus' contemporaries and for
those described in the Acts of the Apostles, even up to Theophilus' time. Whatever keeps these brothers from obedience
to Moses and the prophets will most likely keep them from
obedience to one who has even risen from the dead. Indeed,
what does keep the avaricious from repentance?

17

*Scandal and Forgiveness • Faith and Humility
• Gratitude, the Kingdom and the Day of the
Son of Man*

Given the impact of the Pharisees' lives on their contemporaries, Jesus addresses the seriousness of the evil that
leads others into sin, especially those described as "one of
these little ones," a term which shows Jesus' care for those
who cannot protect themselves. Jesus asks his disciples to
protect themselves from such sinful people.

Jesus also wants his disciples to forgive those who, having hurt his disciples and been reprimanded by them, ask
for forgiveness. Even if this request for forgiveness be made
seven times a day, Jesus wants it given. Such a teaching reveals the value, in Jesus' eyes, of the person who fails many
times, even hurting others, but repents; this is the opposite
kind of person from the one who was just pictured as leading people into sin.

It seems that to ask that a person forgive a brother
seven times a day is something the apostles find impossible;
they suggest this as they ask for "an increase of faith" so as
to be able to live up to what Jesus asks. In other words,
without special gifts they cannot be expected to forgive a
repentant brother seven times a day. The Lord notes simply
that, if they are committed to him, they need no "increase,"
for look what "faith the size of a mustard seed" can do. Their
problem in forgiving others is not to be found in God's not
providing enough help, but in themselves.

The next parable urges obedience to the will of God

17And he said to his disciples, "Temptations to sin are sure to come; but woe to him by whom they come! ²It would be better for him if a millstone were hung round his neck and he were cast into the sea, than that he should cause one of these little ones to sin. ³Take heed to yourselves; if your brother sins, rebuke him, and if he repents, forgive him; ⁴and if he sins against you seven times in the day, and turns to you seven times, and says, 'I repent,' you must forgive him."

5 The apostles said to the Lord, "Increase our faith!" ⁶And the Lord said, "If you had faith as a grain of mustard seed, you could say to this sycamore tree, 'Be rooted up, and be planted in the sea,' and it would obey you.

7 "Will any one of you, who has a servant plowing or keeping sheep, say to him when he has come in from the field, 'Come at once and sit down at table'? ⁸Will he not rather say to him, 'Prepare supper for me, and gird yourself and serve me, till I eat and drink; and afterward you shall eat and drink'? ⁹Does he thank the servant because he did what was commanded? ¹⁰So you also, when you have done all that is commanded you, say, 'We are unworthy servants; we have only done what was our duty.' "

11 On the way to Jerusalem he was passing along between Samaria and Galilee. ¹²And as he entered a village, he was met by ten lepers, who stood at a distance ¹³and lifted up their voices and said, "Jesus, Master, have mercy on us." ¹⁴When he saw them he said to them, "Go and show yourselves to the priests." And as they went they were cleansed. ¹⁵Then one of them, when he saw

that he was healed, turned back, praising God with a loud voice; [16]and he fell on his face at Jesus' feet, giving him thanks. Now he was a Samaritan. [17]Then said Jesus, "Were not ten cleansed? Where are the nine? [18]Was no one found to return and give praise to God except this foreigner?" [19]And he said to him, "Rise and go your way; your faith has made you well."

20 Being asked by the Pharisees when the kingdom of God was coming, he answered them, "The kingdom of God is not coming with signs to be observed; [21]nor will they say, 'Lo, here it is!' or 'There!' for behold, the kingdom of God is in the midst of you."

22 And he said to the disciples, "The days are coming when you will desire to see one of the days of the Son of man, and you will not see it. [23]And they will say to you, 'Lo, there!' or 'Lo, here!' Do not go, do not follow them. [24]For as the lightning flashes and lights up the sky from one side to the other, so will the Son of man be in his day. [25]But first he must suffer many things and be rejected by this generation. [26]As it was in the days of Noah, so will it be in the days of the Son of man. [27]They ate, they drank, they married, they were given in marriage, until the day when Noah entered the ark, and the flood came and destroyed them all. [28]Likewise as it was in the days of Lot—they ate, they drank, they bought, they sold, they planted, they built, [29]but on the day when Lot went out from Sodom fire and sulphur rained from heaven and destroyed them all— [30]so will it be on the day when the Son of man is revealed. [31]On that day, let him who is on the housetop, with his goods in the house, not come down to take them away; and likewise let him who is in the field not turn back. [32]Remember Lot's wife. [33]Whoever seeks to gain his life will lose it, but whoever loses his life will preserve it. [34]I tell you, in that night there will

be two in one bed; one will be taken and the other left. [35]There will be two women grinding together; one will be taken and the other left." [37]And they said to him, "Where, Lord?" He said to them, "Where the body is, there the eagles will be gathered together."

as the ordinary obligation of one who is God's covenant partner. One should not think that God owes him something because he has lived up to his agreement with God. Concretely, let the disciple carry out Jesus' teaching to forgive as often as a truly repentant person asks for it; the disciple is not to claim that God owes him more, that it is God's fault for not being satisfied if the disciple does not live up to the covenant.

It is not the Master who should be grateful to the disciple, but the disciple who should be grateful to the Master. Jesus, Luke notes, is on his way ever closer to Jerusalem, when, at the edge of Samaria (which borders the north of Judea and the south of Galilee), Jesus is asked for pity by ten lepers. Jesus sends them to the priests, those designated by the Mosaic law to declare that a leper was able to return to live among God's people, and along the way to the priests the ten are cured. Wonderful as this miracle was for the total lives for these ten people, the ultimate reason for the inclusion of the story is not the cure: it is the ingratitude of the nine lepers. More accurately, the point of the story is that the nine lepers who were ungrateful to Jesus are precisely those who, because of their special relationship with Yahweh as members of his beloved people, could be expected to return thanks, and be more sensitive to Yahweh's cure through Jesus than this miserable and blasphemous Samaritan, who, according to Jewish perspectives, should get nothing from Yahweh. Jesus is teaching his disciples who—God or the disciples—should be grateful to the other; but through this story, Luke is also subtly recalling that rift between God and his people which ends in the terrible fact that most of God's people, as Luke knew it, were Gentile.

The miracle worked by Jesus for these ten lepers is a manifestation of power associated, in Jewish thinking, with the power of God's kingdom. The Pharisees ask about the time of coming of the fullness, of which this cure is just a beginning: presumably the kingdom will come in the future, and will be an observable and distinctive event, different from what the Pharisees knew by their experiences in this age. Jesus corrects them: the kingdom of God is among them. They need not look to the future, nor for something essentially different from what they now experience: the kingdom is Jesus. Jesus is the fullness of the kingdom; thus, he is able to manifest its characteristics as God wishes. It is the plan of God which has determined when the Messiah, the Son of David on David's throne as Lord at God's right hand, will bring about the fullness of the kingdom. Certainly, the resurrection and ascension of Jesus must come first, as Acts will argue in its second chapter when Peter speaks, but the Jesus who stands before the Pharisees is that one in whose hands the kingdom of God is placed forever. Such had the angel Gabriel indicated to Mary at the annunciation.

What is to come is that period known as the days of the Son of Man, a time in which the kingdom in its fullness will arrive. One will long for one of those days, for they should be days of justice and salvation from evil. Since no one knows when they will come, there is no sense in listening to people who claim to know. Certainly, though, they will occur after the suffering predicted as part of the fate of the Son of Man prior to his exaltation and installation as judge of the entire world.

As in the days of Noah, so in the days of the Son of Man. So suddenly will these days arrive that those ready for them will be the only ones not surprised. Indeed, it is hinted that those who keep their minds and desires fixed only on this age will not only be surprised, but punished, as were those of Noah's time, who likewise were not ready and unworthy for salvation. The days will come so swiftly that one will have no time for change. Where will all this happen, where will they see the Son of Man finally come? The answer is only this: where Jesus is, there you will find all these things occurring.

18

Perseverance, Humility, the Danger of Riches • Jesus Prophesies His Suffering and Cures Blindness

In speaking of the days of the Son of Man, those days involving the judgment of the world by the Son of Man after his humiliation and suffering, Jesus does not reveal the time of these days. This unknown factor leads Jesus to encourage readiness for those days, but also to encourage perseverance, particularly in prayer. Surely this advice of Jesus becomes one of the hallmarks of the early Christian communities Luke describes in Acts. This perseverance Jesus concretizes through a parable in which a judge finally hears the case of a woman simply because of her perseverance.

But the end of the parable looks to other questions than that of perseverance. The woman had pleaded with the judge for justice from her enemies. Jesus notes that God sees the injustices done to his chosen ones and hears their cries for relief; he will deliver his oppressed chosen ones on that great, final day of the Son of Man—but by then, will the Son of Man find that the beloved have still remained faithful? Recall the ending of the Our Father: lead us not into the temptation (which precedes the coming of the Son of Man), but deliver us from the Evil One (who will make his last and most terrible assault on God's beloved before the days of the Son of Man).

Another parable with praying as its context once more calls for real self-appraisal, self-knowledge before God. The parable does not condemn the Pharisee for the good deeds

18And he told them a parable, to the effect that they ought always to pray and not lose heart. ²He said, "In a certain city there was a judge who neither feared God nor regarded man; ³and there was a widow in that city who kept coming to him and saying, 'Vindicate me against my adversary.' ⁴For a while he refused; but afterward he said to himself, 'Though I neither fear God nor regard man, ⁵yet because this widow bothers me, I will vindicate her, or she will wear me out by her continual coming.' " ⁶And the Lord said, "Hear what the unrighteous judge says. ⁷And will not God vindicate his elect, who cry to him day and night? Will he delay long over them? ⁸I tell you, he will vindicate them speedily. Nevertheless, when the Son of man comes, will he find faith on earth?"

9 He also told this parable to some who trusted in themselves that they were righteous and despised others: ¹⁰"Two men went up into the temple to pray, one a Pharisee and the other a tax collector. ¹¹The Pharisee stood and prayed thus with himself, 'God, I thank thee that I am not like other men, extortioners, unjust, adulterers, or even like this tax collector. ¹²I fast twice a week, I give tithes of all that I get.' ¹³But the tax collector, standing far off, would not even lift up his eyes to heaven, but beat his breast, saying, 'God, be merciful to me a sinner!' ¹⁴I tell you, this man went down to his house justified rather than the other; for every one who exalts himself will be humbled, but he who humbles himself will be exalted."

15 Now they were bringing even infants to him that

he might touch them; and when the disciples saw it, they rebuked them. [16]But Jesus called them to him, saying, "Let the children come to me, and do not hinder them; for to such belongs the kingdom of God. [17]Truly, I say to you, whoever does not receive the kingdom of God like a child shall not enter it."

18 And a ruler asked him, "Good Teacher, what shall I do to inherit eternal life?" [19]And Jesus said to him, "Why do you call me good? No one is good but God alone. [20]You know the commandments: 'Do not commit adultery, Do not kill, Do not steal, Do not bear false witness, Honor your father and mother.' " [21]And he said, "All these I have observed from my youth." [22]And when Jesus heard it, he said to him, "One thing you still lack. Sell all that you have and distribute to the poor, and you will have treasure in heaven; and come, follow me." [23]But when he heard this he became sad, for he was very rich. [24]Jesus looking at him said, "How hard it is for those who have riches to enter the kingdom of God! [25]For it is easier for a camel to go through the eye of a needle than for a rich man to enter the kingdom of God." [26]Those who heard it said, "Then who can be saved?" [27]But he said, "What is impossible with men is possible with God." [28]And Peter said, "Lo, we have left our homes and followed you." [29]And he said to them, "Truly, I say to you, there is no man who has left house or wife or brothers or parents or children, for the sake of the kingdom of God, [30]who will not receive manifold more in this time, and in the age to come eternal life."

31 And taking the twelve, he said to them, "Behold, we are going up to Jerusalem, and everything that is written of the Son of man by the prophets will be accomplished. [32]For he will be delivered to the Gentiles, and will be mocked and shamefully treated and spit upon;

³³they will scourge him and kill him, and on the third day he will rise." ³⁴But they understood none of these things; this saying was hid from them, and they did not grasp what was said.

35 As he drew near to Jericho, a blind man was sitting by the roadside begging; ³⁶and hearing a multitude going by, he inquired what this meant. ³⁷They told him, "Jesus of Nazareth is passing by." ³⁸And he cried, "Jesus, Son of David, have mercy on me!" ³⁹And those who were in front rebuked him, telling him to be silent; but he cried out all the more, "Son of David, have mercy on me!" ⁴⁰And Jesus stopped, and commanded him to be brought to him; and when he came near, he asked him, ⁴¹"What do you want me to do for you?" He said, "Lord, let me receive my sight." ⁴²And Jesus said to him, "Receive your sight; your faith has made you well." ⁴³And immediately he received his sight and followed him, glorifying God; and all the people, when they saw it, gave praise to God.

he does, but for his self-exaltation; in other words, he can tell God of his good actions, but he should let God be the judge of them in the context of the Pharisee's total self, for it is likely that the Pharisee is not concerned to speak of his sins; he only wants to exalt himself, sell himself to God. Jesus prefers, not the sinfulness of the tax collector, but his recognition of his true image before God and his throwing himself on God's mercy. This sinner God can lift up; the Pharisee has given God no opening, but reveals the kind of attitude—that of self-glorification, particularly through depreciation of a fellow human being—that encourages God to "bring the Pharisee to a knowledge of his need for God" through humiliation.

Luke puts next a story about little children, to whom one can compare the attitudes of the previous adults, the Pharisee and the tax collector. It is to the humble, the little ones, that the kingdom of God belongs; if the adult does not become humble, he will never enter it.

But the fullness of happiness is, for the Christian, to be achieved mysteriously through the following of Christ and not simply in the fulfillment of the law of Moses—mysteriously, for though one does all that God asks, he will find that something is still missing. It is union with Jesus Christ. It is to this union that the entire New Testament gives witness, including of course the Acts of the Apostles. Ultimately, it is union with Jesus which offers the fullest happiness, though there is no denying that obedience to God's will shall bring a person to entry into the kingdom.

One can understand this story of the rich man as a subtle argument that the way of the New Testament is better than the way of the Mosaic law. One thing is lacking to the law and that is what Christianity has—Christ. But the story is more than a polemic; it suggests that eternal life is to be found ultimately in the company of Christ, that nothing of this world is to be desired in preference to Jesus.

Unfortunately, the rich man prefers his riches to walking with Jesus to Jerusalem; he is willing to separate himself from Jesus for the sake of his riches, even though he is promised greater riches some day. A great sadness fills the rich man, for he must admit that the possession of riches which separate him from Christ's company is no gift to his peace and happiness.

Jesus, too, realizes the opportunity this man has sacrificed to hold on to his riches and draws the conclusion, based on experience, that love of possessions will keep many a person from letting God's mind rule him, from the kingdom of God. He adds, however, rather cryptically, that whereas man will usually lose out to wealth and be dominated by it to his loss of salvation, God will intervene to reverse this "usual" loss. God will fight to win human beings who hold on to possessions.

Peter, aware that he and his companions have indeed left all to follow Jesus, puts into words what bothers everybody: "What about us?" Jesus can only spell out in more extravagant terms than those he used with the rich man that the treasures stored up for those who have given up their treasures to follow Jesus are immense: recompense many times over, both in this life and in the life to come. In some way not explained here, to die to follow Jesus results in an immensely greater enjoyment of life than does the retention of possessions coupled with rejection of Jesus' company.

To speak of renunciation, of dispossessing one's self, is to speak of death—and this brings Luke to introduce, on the heels of Jesus' request that people "die" to their wealth for him, the third announcement that Jesus must die, in Jerusalem, and rise from the dead to live again. Jesus is ever

more precise in his details about his future suffering, a fact
which suggests to some interpreters that Luke has, from his
knowledge of how Jesus actually was mistreated, taken a
more vague prophecy of suffering from Jesus and made it
into a more specific forecast. Luke certainly does underline
the inability of the disciples to grasp at all what Jesus is
promising about himself; not only can they not believe that
he will be overcome by his enemies, but they recognize no
necessity in the prophets that all this must happen.

Perhaps it is in light of the disciples' inability to see that
Luke adds now the story of the man cured of blindness at
the entry to Jericho (about ten miles due east of Jerusalem).
Certainly the blind man has shown persistence in his belief
that it is Jesus who can give him sight; Jesus affirms that it
is the man's trust in Jesus, and not in someone else, which
has led to this man's being saved from his life of blindness.
Will the disciples trust in Jesus for understanding of the
truth of things?

19

Jesus Meets Zacchaeus, Tells the Parable of the Pounds ● The Messiah Descends Toward Jerusalem and Enters the Temple

Jesus has, at least in the last miles of the journey to Jerusalem (and to the right hand of his Father), followed the Jordan River to Jericho. Amidst the crowds who gather around him Jesus spies a man called Zacchaeus who, because of his short height, had climbed a sycamore tree to get a glimpse of Jesus. The enduring element of the story lies in Jesus' willingness, proved so often before this, to address himself to sinners in the hope that they will repent. Zacchaeus was no "ordinary" tax collector, but was a regional director of a number of tax collectors; if the ordinary tax collector was presumed to be crooked, Zacchaeus was crooked *par excellence*. Jesus is willing to go into the sinners' homes and eat with them, in the hope that his love might move them to repent. Zacchaeus does, in fact, repent; this is shown by the amends he is willing to make, for he imposes on himself fines which are the highest demanded by Jewish and Roman law.

The crowd had complained about Jesus' willingness to associate with Zacchaeus, but Jesus, at the end of the story, can say that salvation has come to this house. Jesus came for this purpose and came away victorious, for he won the repentance which involves salvation. As part of his commitment to the children of Israel, Jesus seeks out even those children who are lost. He has found what was lost, he has saved it!

19 He entered Jericho and was passing through. ²And there was a man named Zacchaeus; he was a chief tax collector, and rich. ³And he sought to see who Jesus was, but could not, on account of the crowd, because he was small of stature. ⁴So he ran on ahead and climbed up into a sycamore tree to see him, for he was to pass that way. ⁵And when Jesus came to the place, he looked up and said to him, "Zacchaeus, make haste and come down; for I must stay at your house today." ⁶So he made haste and came down, and received him joyfully. ⁷And when they saw it they all murmured, "He has gone in to be the guest of a man who is a sinner." ⁸And Zacchaeus stood and said to the Lord, "Behold, Lord, the half of my goods I give to the poor; and if I have defrauded any one of anything, I restore it fourfold." ⁹And Jesus said to him, "Today salvation has come to this house, since he also is a son of Abraham. ¹⁰For the Son of man came to seek and to save the lost."

11 As they heard these things, he proceeded to tell a parable, because he was near to Jerusalem, and because they supposed that the kingdom of God was to appear immediately. ¹²He said therefore, "A nobleman went into a far country to receive a kingdom and then return. ¹³Calling ten of his servants, he gave them ten pounds, and said to them, 'Trade with these till I come.' ¹⁴But his citizens hated him and sent an embassy after him, saying, 'We do not want this man to reign over us.' ¹⁵When he returned, having received the kingdom, he commanded these servants, to whom he had given the money, to be called to him, that he might know what they had gained

by trading. [16]The first came before him, saying, 'Lord, your pound has made ten pounds more.' [17]And he said to him, 'Well done, good servant! Because you have been faithful in a very little, you shall have authority over ten cities.' [18]And the second came, saying, 'Lord, your pound has made five pounds.' [19]And he said to him, 'And you are to be over five cities.' [20]Then another came, saying, 'Lord, here is your pound, which I kept laid away in a napkin; [21]for I was afraid of you, because you are a severe man; you take up what you did not lay down, and reap what you did not sow.' [22]He said to him, 'I will condemn you out of your own mouth, you wicked servant! You knew that I was a severe man, taking up what I did not lay down and reaping what I did not sow? [23]Why then did you not put my money into the bank, and at my coming I should have collected it with interest?' [24]And he said to those who stood by, 'Take the pound from him, and give it to him who has the ten pounds.' [25](And they said to him, 'Lord, he has ten pounds!') [26]"I tell you, that to every one who has will more be given; but from him who has not, even what he has will be taken away. [27]But as for these enemies of mine, who did not want me to reign over them, bring them here and slay them before me.' "

28 And when he had said this, he went on ahead, going up to Jerusalem. [29]When he drew near to Bethphage and Bethany, at the mount that is called Olivet, he sent two of the disciples, [30]saying, "Go into the village opposite, where on entering you will find a colt tied, on which no one has ever yet sat; untie it and bring it here. [31]If any one asks you, 'Why are you untying it?' you shall say this, 'The Lord has need of it.' " [32]So those who were sent went away and found it as he had told them. [33]And as they were untying the colt, its owners said to them, "Why are you untying the colt?" [34]And they said, "The

Lord has need of it." ³⁵And they brought it to Jesus, and throwing their garments on the colt they set Jesus upon it. ³⁶And as he rode along, they spread their garments on the road. ³⁷As he was now drawing near, at the descent of the Mount of Olives, the whole multitude of the disciples began to rejoice and praise God with a loud voice for all the mighty works that they had seen, ³⁸saying, "Blessed is the King who comes in the name of the Lord! Peace in heaven and glory in the highest!" ³⁹And some of the Pharisees in the multitude said to him, "Teacher, rebuke your disciples." ⁴⁰He answered, "I tell you, if these were silent, the very stones would cry out."

41 And when he drew near and saw the city he wept over it, ⁴²saying, "Would that even today you knew the things that make for peace! But now they are hid from your eyes. ⁴³For the days shall come upon you, when your enemies will cast up a bank about you and surround you, and hem you in on every side, ⁴⁴and dash you to the ground, you and your children within you, and they will not leave one stone upon another in you; because you did not know the time of your visitation."

45 And he entered the temple and began to drive out those who sold, ⁴⁶saying to them, "It is written, 'My house shall be a house of prayer'; but you have made it a den of robbers."

47 And he was teaching daily in the temple. The chief priests and the scribes and the principal men of the people sought to destroy him; ⁴⁸but they did not find anything they could do, for all the people hung upon his words.

Jesus is now wending his way up from Jericho toward the Mount of Olives, some ten miles distant from Jericho. Though Luke had noted at the beginning of Jesus' journey to Jerusalem that Jesus was on his way to his Father, Luke now makes it clear that the crowds with Jesus expect him to introduce the kingdom of God when he enters Jerusalem. (Note that, after Jesus fails to do this at his entrance to Jerusalem, his disciples expect him to do it before his ascension, in Acts 1:6.) In light of the crowd's expectation, but also as a teaching for later disciples like Theophilus, Jesus constructs a parable of various significant elements. First, there is the "man of noble birth" who goes to a distant country to become king; he will return. This is Jesus, and his compatriots, who detest him and refuse him as king, are those Jews of the Acts of the Apostles who continue to reject Jesus as Messiah, descendant of David. Since it was customary that kings rid themselves of opponents in most drastic manners, it is not surprising that Jesus, who started the parable with the imagery of kingship as it was experienced in his day, should conclude the parable still remaining faithful to that imagery; the king's return is the eventual return of the Messiah Lord from his Father's right hand to judge Israel and all the nations.

Second, there is the work to be done by ten servants during the absence of the king; this is the work of loving God and loving one's neighbor through gifts by which one can contribute to the growth of the household or Christian community; the motivation as to why one servant does not use his gift is not pertinent to Jesus' teaching, but the fact that the servant did not use his gift for the good of the community is very pertinent to Jesus' lesson. Jesus had taught in an earlier parable that "when a man has had a great deal given him, a great deal will be demanded of him; when a man has had a great deal given him on trust, even more will be expected of him" (Lk 12:48). He underlines that teaching as he looks ever more to the life of the Christian communities which will develop while he is absent.

Jesus is just about at the top of the Mount of Olives and therefore just about in sight of the city and its temple, less than a mile from the top of the Mount. Jesus, by asking for a colt to ride down to the gates of Jerusalem, strongly suggests that he is indeed the Messiah, for to ride this colt, amidst the expectations of the crowds, is to recall to them the prophecy: Jerusalem, see your king coming to you, humble and on the colt of an ass (Zec 9:9). The crowd fails to grasp that the Messiahship of Jesus is laced with humility, with meekness; to have such a Messiah is a bitter lesson still to be learned.

Almost as a conclusion to all he has reported, Luke notes the crowd's praise of God for "all the miracles they have seen." The Galilee period is over; we are in a new phase of Jesus' ministry. Their song of praise echoes Jesus' riding on the colt: he is the king who comes as representative of God; heaven is no longer angry with earth, and the highest heaven, where God lives, is filled with cries of God's gloriousness. To the Pharisees who resent and deny the claim of Jesus to kingship, Jesus can only reply that nature itself will proclaim him, if they succeed in silencing his disciples. Jesus indeed, by his kingly gesture and amidst the cries of the crowd, is proclaiming his kingship over Jerusalem and the temple and wants his claim to be accepted. It is the will of men which will thwart his claim. To silence his followers will not negate the truth.

Coming down the Mount of Olives toward the Kidron Valley and the eastern wall of Jerusalem, Jesus begins to weep over the city upon which he gazes. He sees linked together the rejection of himself and the destruction of the city. In this Jesus reflects that age-old understanding that the destruction of God's city is always due to its disobedience to him, apart from questions of armies and power and defense and political alliances. (Note that the detail in the description of Jerusalem's fate is a major reason why scholars say that Luke's Gospel was written after the destruction of Jerusalem in 70 A.D.—the details are put in by Luke after 70 A.D. in light of what he learned after the sad event.)

Luke never says that Jesus entered Jerusalem, the city; Jesus is only placed in the temple area (which is slightly larger than a football field and contains an oblong building—west to east—which is divided into three parts, the most westerly part being the most holy place on earth). Most scholars presume that Luke intentionally kept Jesus out of Jerusalem, for it is the city which rejects all the prophets and is therefore to be rejected itself. Acts, however, will pick up with the preaching about Jesus in Jerusalem.

To say that Jesus drove out sellers who were "in the Temple" is to say that Jesus drove out those who were selling animals, etc. (for use in temple sacrifices) from the area of the temple grounds which lie to the north of the temple building itself; in brief, "temple" may refer to the central building of worship or may refer to the large courtyard (or precincts, or platform or esplanade) which surrounds the central building on its north, east and south sides. Surrounding the entire temple area or courtyard or precinct is a wall with an overhang or roof supported by pillars. Under this overhang Jesus would teach—and later his disciples would gather after Pentecost.

That Jesus drove out the sellers in the temple area was a gesture of a prophet by which Jesus tried to underline his sensitivity to the misuse of the temple area—an area which should be kept for prayer, not for selling, even of things necessary for temple sacrifice. In a crowded precinct his gesture was significant and startling, but hardly unique to the ways of prophets.

Jesus immediately begins his usual chore of teaching; some of his teachings we will learn very soon. At the moment, Luke highlights the difference of reactions: the leaders want to get rid of Jesus, whereas the simple people hang on his every word (and they are the most trustworthy). Luke also introduces new opponents of Jesus: the chief priests, those seven or eight men, often relatives of the high priest, who run the huge complex known as the temple. Leading, wealthy citizens are also coming forward in opposition to Jesus.

20

Jesus Is Challenged by the Chief Priests, the Scribes and the Sadducees • Then Challenges and Criticizes the Scribes

Jesus continues teaching in the temple area and continues to proclaim the good news of salvation. Chief priests, scribes and elders (the chief priests, some scribes and some elders, or traditionally wealthy Jews, make up the Sanhedrin or ruling body of seventy members over Israel) demand from Jesus to know by what authority he teaches. The outcome of their demand is a stand-off, but what Luke underlines again is the unwillingness of Jewish authorities (earlier it had been Pharisees) to accept the call to repentance, whether that of John or that of Jesus.

It is obvious from their approach and whole manner that these leaders of Israel were interested and determined to get rid of Jesus. Their attitude leads Jesus to tell a stinging parable—ostensibly for the people, but quite clearly aimed at the leaders of Israel, in whose hands rests the fate of the nation.

The parable is rather straightforward and clear; God, the owner of a vineyard (Jerusalem/Israel is often described as a vineyard in Old Testament poetry), sends various prophets to demand from those responsible for the vineyard the fruit of the vineyard. The Old Testament is witness to the many prophets Israel has sternly rejected. Now God sends his only Son to reap the fruit of repentance—only to have him thrown out of the vineyard and killed. All attention is now drawn to the owner of the vineyard: What will he do?

SCRIPTURE TEXT

20 One day, as he was teaching the people in the temple and preaching the gospel, the chief priests and the scribes with the elders came up ²and said to him, "Tell us by what authority you do these things, or who it is that gave you this authority." ³He answered them, "I also will ask you a question; now tell me, ⁴Was the baptism of John from heaven or from men?" ⁵And they discussed it with one another, saying, "If we say, 'From heaven,' he will say, 'Why did you not believe him?' ⁶But if we say, 'From men,' all the people will stone us; for they are convinced that John was a prophet." ⁷So they answered that they did not know whence it was. ⁸And Jesus said to them, "Neither will I tell you by what authority I do these things."

9 And he began to tell the people this parable: "A man planted a vineyard, and let it out to tenants, and went into another country for a long while. ¹⁰When the time came, he sent a servant to the tenants, that they should give him some of the fruit of the vineyard; but the tenants beat him, and sent him away empty-handed. ¹¹And he sent another servant; him also they beat and treated shamefully, and sent him away empty-handed. ¹²And he sent yet a third; this one they wounded and cast out. ¹³Then the owner of the vineyard said, 'What shall I do? I will send my beloved son; it may be they will respect him.' ¹⁴But when the tenants saw him, they said to themselves, 'This is the heir; let us kill him, that the inheritance may be ours.' ¹⁵And they cast him out of the vineyard and killed him. What then will the owner of the vineyard do to them? ¹⁶He will come and destroy those

tenants, and give the vineyard to others." When they heard this, they said, "God forbid!" [17]But he looked at them and said, "What then is this that is written:

'The very stone which the builders rejected
has become the head of the corner'?

[18]Every one who falls on that stone will be broken to pieces; but when it falls on any one it will crush him."

19 The scribes and the chief priests tried to lay hands on him at that very hour, but they feared the people; for they perceived that he had told this parable against them. [20]So they watched him, and sent spies, who pretended to be sincere, that they might take hold of what he said, so as to deliver him up to the authority and jurisdiction of the governor. [21]They asked him, "Teacher, we know that you speak and teach rightly, and show no partiality, but truly teach the way of God. [22]Is it lawful for us to give tribute to Caesar, or not?" [23]But he perceived their craftiness, and said to them, [24]"Show me a coin. Whose likeness and inscription has it?" They said, "Caesar's." [25]He said to them, "Then render to Caesar the things that are Caesar's, and to God the things that are God's." [26]And they were not able in the presence of the people to catch him by what he said; but marveling at his answer they were silent.

27 There came to him some Sadducees, those who say that there is no resurrection, [28]and they asked him a question, saying, "Teacher, Moses wrote for us that if a man's brother dies, having a wife but no children, the man must take the wife and raise up children for his brother. [29]Now there were seven brothers; the first took a wife, and died without children; [30]and the second [31]and the third took her, and likewise all seven left no children and died. [32]Afterward the woman also died. [33]In the resur-

rection, therefore, whose wife will the woman be? For the seven had her as wife."

34 And Jesus said to them, "The sons of this age marry and are given in marriage; [35]but those who are accounted worthy to attain to that age and to the resurrection from the dead neither marry nor are given in marriage, [36]for they cannot die any more, because they are equal to angels and are sons of God, being sons of the resurrection. [37]But that the dead are raised, even Moses showed, in the passage about the bush, where he calls the Lord the God of Abraham and the God of Isaac and the God of Jacob. [38]Now he is not God of the dead, but of the living; for all live to him." [39]And some of the scribes answered, "Teacher, you have spoken well." [40]For they no longer dared to ask him any question.

41 But he said to them, "How can they say that the Christ is David's son? [42]For David himself says in the Book of Psalms,

'The Lord said to my Lord,
    Sit at my right hand,
[43]till I make thy enemies a stool for thy feet.'
[44]David thus calls him Lord; so how is he his son?"

45 And in the hearing of all the people he said to his disciples, [46]"Beware of the scribes, who like to go about in long robes, and love salutations in the market places and the best seats in the synagogues and the places of honor at feasts, [47]who devour widows' houses and for a pretense make long prayers. They will receive the greater condemnation."

The answer to this question is not simply that God will punish Israel. One must be more precise and say that the opportunity for repentance and salvation will now be given to others than Israel, that there will be another group to work the vineyard and to produce the fruits God wants. This parable warns the people of Israel, and especially those responsible for them, that God will look elsewhere for his covenant partner, should Israel remain unrepentant. The Old Testament quotation underscores this threat: what Israel has rejected will become the very foundation of a new people of God, i.e., there will arise a people whose very essence and existence is founded on their belief in that Jesus, rejected by Israel, who calls for repentance, assures forgiveness and in certain ways already expresses the kingdom of God. Through him will the kingdom of God come, and only through him, for God has so decreed.

Eager to stop such talk, the Jewish leaders look for opportunities whereby they might, through Jesus' own mistakes, make the people disillusioned about Jesus and thus make his death more acceptable to all. One opportunity they manufacture is this, to make Jesus either defend Caesar and thus incur the wrath of the enslaved of Jerusalem, or deny Caesar and thus give pretext for reporting him to the Roman authorities. Thus, they put before Jesus the question: Is it permissible to pay taxes to Caesar or not? Indeed, most of Jesus' listeners were paying over thirty-five percent of their wages to Caesar!

Jesus' answer is one that delivers him neither to Pilate nor to the crowds. All Jesus does is uphold a principle which everyone admits to be true, particularly those whose lives are based on the teachings of Moses: if something belongs to somebody, give it to him. Jesus makes no attempt to argue that the coin with Caesar's image on it is Caesar's, much less to argue that Jews should pay taxes to Rome; if anything, he

makes the Jews admit that the coin has an image on it that
might suggest that the coin belongs rightfully to Caesar and
should be given to him. But Jesus does not decide the issue
of taxes. What is of equal importance for Jesus is that the
question—and his answer—gives him the opportunity once
again to ask that God be given what belongs to God. Here,
too, Jesus does not specify what is God's, but he does underline the rightness of giving to God what is his.

At this point Luke takes a moment to note that the Sanhedrin members, as a group, speak no more. By this note
the reader should be aware that the verbal conflict is by and
large over; the next stage is imminent. And there must be
a "next stage," even though they were unable to find fault
with anything Jesus said, and thus had no grounds for trying
Jesus.

There remains one group of religious authority in Israel
which has not had a direct confrontation with Jesus; this is
the group known as the Sadducees. The Sadducees, like the
Pharisees, originated about two hundred years before Jesus;
unlike the Pharisees, they accepted only the first five books
of the Old Testament as truly binding and most holy. Under
a very conservative reading of these five books of Moses
they drew the conclusion that, among other things, there is
no resurrection from the dead, no afterlife with God. Most
high priests, chief priests and wealthy Jews were Sadducean
in theology; it is, then, fitting that we meet them at this
point.

The Sadducees present Jesus with a problem which they
think will discredit the whole idea of an afterlife. The problem is based upon a provision of the Mosaic law which tries
to ensure that the property of a man who dies without an
heir will, nonetheless, be safely handed on to an heir. How
does the law provide for this? A near-relative of the deceased
is obliged to marry the widow with the hope that thereby

will an heir to the deceased be raised up. Such was the importance of maintaining intact every man's inheritable property! Now, the Sadducees so arrange their story that, by the time the widow dies, she has had six marriages besides her marriage to her original husband. The problem lies in this: Whose wife will she be in the afterlife? The underlying question is: Does not our own Mosaic law suggest that the afterlife is ridiculous?

Jesus answers both the problem and the underlying question. Accepting the limitations of the Sadducean story, Jesus notes that, since there is no death in the afterlife, the original husband will not be dead and thus will not have need for his relatives to take his place as husband of his wife. Jesus then points to Scripture, which the Sadducees accept, which asserts that God *is* the God of Abraham, Isaac and Jacob. Much emphasis is put on that word *is*, for God is affirming to Moses (who lived hundreds of years after the deaths of Abraham, Isaac and Jacob) that he *is* the God of the patriarchs—not "was." Scripture can only be interpreted as meaning that God, centuries after the deaths of the three patriarchs, remains their God, that they still remain as his subjects—thus, they are alive, for it makes no sense for God to affirm himself to be now before Moses a God of people who exist no more.

It is worth pointing out in regard to this Sadducean encounter that the way Luke retells this Marcan story stresses the point that one must be worthy to enter this afterlife; again, Jesus in Luke is not content to win an argument, but must endeavor to call his fellow Jews to repentance.

Scribes, those well acquainted with the law, praise Jesus' arguments, particularly his use of Scripture. Jesus takes a turn now and asks the scribes to put themselves to the test and answer a problem Jesus founds on Scripture. According

to Scripture, the Messiah (= Christ) is to be a descendant
of David; this implies that the Messiah is a dependent of
David and will come sometime after David. Yet, this very
David says in one of his poems (Jews at Jesus' time thought
David wrote all the Psalms) that the Lord Yahweh said to
David's Lord (= Messiah) to sit at Yahweh's right hand; thus,
David's own words suggest that the Messiah is greater than
David (he is David's Lord) and even prior to David. If the
Messiah is David's Lord, how can he be his son? Luke leaves
this question hanging in the air; its answer points the way
to an ever deeper understanding of that person who is both
Lord and Messiah.

The scribes are those who know the law; their knowledge should be a help to their fellow Jews, but it is not. The
scribes seek only their own advantage, their own self-glory,
even at the expense of others. More severe will be the judgment God brings upon them.

21

*A Widow Gives Her All • Jesus Speaks of the
Destruction of Jerusalem and Thereafter •
Jesus Spends His Last Days Teaching*

Having just spoken of those who "swallow up the possessions of widows," Jesus now sees a widow putting into
the temple treasury two small coins which, Jesus says, are
"all she had to live on." Is this money that the scribes could
have saved this woman if they had been concerned about
her enough to have interpreted for her what God truly asked
of her? Certainly, the woman stands out for her total generosity; the poor give their all, while the rich give much,
but not all, to God. Coming, as this story does, at the end
of so many teachings and lessons of Jesus regarding generosity toward God and one's neighbor and the lack thereof
on the part of many human beings, particularly the wealthy,
the widow seems to sum up for Jesus that degree of love of
God which he has tried to teach and live out himself. Her
contribution is the greatest, if one measures the heart and
not the value written on the coins.

It was on one of the days of Jesus' teaching in the temple area that his disciples struck up a conversation about
the magnificence of the temple building; indeed, descriptions of the artistry involved in the efforts of Herod the
Great (died 4 B.C.) continued on past Jesus' own days as
thousands of workmen labored to embellish the temple and
its furnishings. For people who lived extremely simple lives,
the gold and silver and precious woods and stones, immense
and beautifully dressed, all must have been a source of won-

SCRIPTURE TEXT

21 He looked up and saw the rich putting their gifts into the treasury; [2]and he saw a poor widow put in two copper coins. [3]And he said, "Truly I tell you, this poor widow has put in more than all of them; [4]for they all contributed out of their abundance, but she out of her poverty put in all the living that she had."

5 And as some spoke of the temple, how it was adorned with noble stones and offerings, he said, [6]"As for these things which you see, the days will come when there shall not be left here one stone upon another that will not be thrown down." [7]And they asked him, "Teacher, when will this be, and what will be the sign when this is about to take place?" [8]And he said, "Take heed that you are not led astray; for many will come in my name, saying, 'I am he!' and, 'The time is at hand!' Do not go after them. [9]And when you hear of wars and tumults, do not be terrified; for this must first take place, but the end will not be at once."

10 Then he said to them, "Nation will rise against nation, and kingdom against kingdom; [11]there will be great earthquakes, and in various places famines and pestilences; and there will be terrors and great signs from heaven. [12]But before all this they will lay their hands on you and persecute you, delivering you up to the synagogues and prisons, and you will be brought before kings and governors for my name's sake. [13]This will be a time for you to bear testimony. [14]Settle it therefore in your minds, not to meditate beforehand how to answer; [15]for I will give you a mouth and wisdom, which none of your adversaries will be able to withstand or contradict. [16]You

will be delivered up even by parents and brothers and kinsmen and friends, and some of you they will put to death; [17]you will be hated by all for my name's sake. [18]But not a hair of your head will perish. [19]By your endurance you will gain your lives.

20 "But when you see Jerusalem surrounded by armies, then know that its desolation has come near. [21]Then let those who are in Judea flee to the mountains, and let those who are inside the city depart, and let not those who are out in the country enter it; [22]for these are days of vengeance, to fulfil all that is written. [23]Alas for those who are with child and for those who give suck in those days! For great distress shall be upon the earth and wrath upon this people; [24]they will fall by the edge of the sword, and be led captive among all nations; and Jerusalem will be trodden down by the Gentiles, until the times of the Gentiles are fulfilled.

25 "And there will be signs in sun and moon and stars, and upon the earth distress of nations in perplexity at the roaring of the sea and the waves, [26]men fainting with fear and with foreboding of what is coming on the world; for the powers of the heavens will be shaken. [27]And then they will see the Son of man coming in a cloud with power and great glory. [28]Now when these things begin to take place, look up and raise your heads, because your redemption is drawing near."

29 And he told them a parable: "Look at the fig tree, and all the trees; [30]as soon as they come out in leaf, you see for yourselves and know that the summer is already near. [31]So also, when you see these things taking place, you know that the kingdom of God is near. [32]Truly, I say to you, this generation will not pass away till all has taken place. [33]Heaven and earth will pass away, but my words will not pass away.

34 "But take heed to yourselves lest your hearts be weighed down with dissipation and drunkenness and cares of this life, and that day come upon you suddenly like a snare; [35]for it will come upon all who dwell upon the face of the whole earth. [36]But watch at all times, praying that you may have strength to escape all these things that will take place, and to stand before the Son of man."

37 And every day he was teaching in the temple, but at night he went out and lodged on the mount called Olivet. [38]And early in the morning all the people came to him in the temple to hear him.

der and excitement never seen otherwise in their whole
lives. It was with numbing shock that the disciples hear Jesus
say that the time is coming when no stone will stand on top
of another, that all this will be destroyed. Jesus is speaking
of the destruction of Jerusalem, and his disciples put to him
the two essential questions which affect themselves: When
will this destruction come? What signs will there be, so we
will be forewarned and thus escape?

What the disciples ask for and what Jesus wants to talk
about do not coincide perfectly. Jesus will talk about the
destruction of Jerusalem, but he wants to put it into a larger
framework, that of the course of history which, while ab-
sorbing the destruction of Jerusalem and other events as
well, culminates in the appearance of the Son of Man coming
in a cloud with power and great glory; Jesus looks from this
moment to the end of this world and the beginning of the
fullness of God's kingdom.

The method of the speech is to speak for four verses
of that series of events, affecting all the elements of this
world we experience (vv 8–11), then to speak of concrete
expectations of events (including the destruction of Jerusalem) the disciples will themselves most surely encounter
(vv 12–24), and finally to return to the conclusion of the
description of signs and events of the entire cosmos as they
lead up to and end with the wonderful appearance of the
Son of Man. Thus, the destruction of Jerusalem, and other
chilling events the disciples must face (as will be described
in part in Acts), are all part of that immense struggle between good and evil which will culminate, optimistically, in
the liberation of those who remain faithful to Jesus.

To the basic description of history leading up to the
appearance of the Son of Man is added a parable about how
one recognizes the nearness of summer by noticing the bud-
ding of trees. So, one will, through experience of these

events foretold in vv 12–24, know that the kingdom of God
in its fullness is not far away; indeed, the disciples will live
through such things as imprisonment and trial for Jesus'
name, betrayal, hatred and death, and the grim encirclement
of Jerusalem announcing the moment of God's vengeance
for its hard-heartedness.

Jesus' last words are an assurance that what he says will
happen will happen, and a pressing encouragement to so
live their lives in prayer and conscious union with God that
they will survive the agonies which will face every human
being, and particularly those who profess the name of Jesus.

The end of Jesus' active life of preaching and teaching
has come. Luke concludes it all by the simple and gener-
alizing report that Jesus continues to teach in the temple
area, and he is listened to from earliest morning. Luke has
spent a long time in outlining the major teachings of Jesus;
when the references are made to "what Jesus taught" in Acts,
one is expected to revert to the Gospel to recall what concretely the teaching is. Essentially, Jesus' teaching has gone
in two directions. There is the teaching which touches upon
the necessity of his death and resurrection, his sitting at the
right hand of his Father in Lordship, as the Son of David
whom God promised would someday sit on David's throne
(= Messiah). Then there is the teaching regarding love of
God and love of neighbor, teaching which reveals God's love
for the poor and afflicted, his disdain for hypocrisy in one's
life before him, the value of each human being and the immense love each person must have for another, the dangers
which threaten to remove God from being my God, to replace him with other gods, like money, the need for perseverance in acts which are befitting repentance, particularly
the need to stay praying and full of unending trust in God.

Luke, like the other evangelists, has laid the groundwork
for the terrible events now to follow. From all that has gone

before one is to make sense out of the ignominy, accusations, pain, betrayal and death—and resurrection—which Luke now describes.

This is a good moment to ask ourselves if Luke has succeeded thus far in his writing so as to help Theophilus grasp the sureness and reliability of the things he has been taught; all Luke has done so far is for that purpose.

22

The Plot Ripens; Jesus at His Last Supper, in the Garden • Peter Denies Jesus, Who Is Mocked and Tried by Jewish Authorities

Passover is the Jewish feast which celebrates the fact that the Angel of Death "passed over" those houses which had sprinkled on their doorposts the blood of a lamb. These houses belonged to the Israelites who lived in Egypt under the cruel Pharaoh, who, despite many signs God worked through Moses and Aaron, would not let God's people go free. A last sign from God was the death of all the first-born in Egypt, of man and beast; only those in Egypt who had the blood of a lamb on their doorposts would not be visited by the Angel of Death. The feast of Passover which Jesus is now to celebrate with his co-religionists recalls that sign, that blood, that lamb, that freedom from slavery, that exodus, that trek through the desert to the land bequeathed centuries earlier to the father of Israel, Abraham.

About the same moment of the year in which Passover was celebrated occurred the beginning of the spring harvest; the first gesture of this annual event was to take grain mixed with water, but without yeast or leaven, and offer this mixture to God in gratitude for the rest of the harvest—which, too, belongs to God, since he produced it on his land, but which is understood to be given to man for his sustenance.

It is at the time of these two feasts, now celebrated together, that Satan, who Luke said was waiting to return at the appointed time (Lk 4:13), enters into Judas—and Judas fulfills the hopes of the chief priests and scribes who were

22 Now the feast of Unleavened Bread drew near, which is called the Passover. ²And the chief priests and the scribes were seeking how to put him to death; for they feared the people.

3 Then Satan entered into Judas called Iscariot, who was of the number of the twelve; ⁴he went away and conferred with the chief priests and officers how he might betray him to them. ⁵And they were glad, and engaged to give him money. ⁶So he agreed, and sought an opportunity to betray him to them in the absence of the multitude.

7 Then came the day of Unleavened Bread, on which the passover lamb had to be sacrificed. ⁸So Jesus sent Peter and John, saying, "Go and prepare the passover for us, that we may eat it." ⁹They said to him, "Where will you have us prepare it?" ¹⁰He said to them, "Behold, when you have entered the city, a man carrying a jar of water will meet you; follow him into the house which he enters, ¹¹and tell the householder, 'The Teacher says to you, Where is the guest room, where I am to eat the passover with my disciples?' ¹²And he will show you a large upper room furnished; there make ready." ¹³And they went, and found it as he had told them; and they prepared the passover.

14 And when the hour came, he sat at table, and the apostles with him. ¹⁵And he said to them, "I have earnestly desired to eat this passover with you before I suffer; ¹⁶for I tell you I shall not eat it until it is fulfilled in the kingdom of God." ¹⁷And he took a cup, and when he had given thanks he said, "Take this, and divide it among

yourselves; ¹⁸for I tell you that from now on I shall not drink of the fruit of the vine until the kingdom of God comes." ¹⁹And he took bread, and when he had given thanks he broke it and gave it to them, saying, "This is my body which is given for you. Do this in remembrance of me." ²⁰And likewise the cup after supper, saying, "This cup which is poured out for you is the new covenant in my blood. ²¹But behold the hand of him who betrays me is with me on the table. ²²For the Son of man goes as it has been determined; but woe to that man by whom he is betrayed!" ²³And they began to question one another, which of them it was that would do this.

24 A dispute also arose among them, which of them was to be regarded as the greatest. ²⁵And he said to them, "The kings of the Gentiles exercise lordship over them; and those in authority over them are called benefactors. ²⁶But not so with you; rather let the greatest among you become as the youngest, and the leader as one who serves. ²⁷For which is the greater, one who sits at table, or one who serves? Is it not the one who sits at table? But I am among you as one who serves.

28 "You are those who have continued with me in my trials; ²⁹and I assign to you, as my Father assigned to me, a kingdom, ³⁰that you may eat and drink at my table in my kingdom, and sit on thrones judging the twelve tribes of Israel.

31 "Simon, Simon, behold, Satan demanded to have you, that he might sift you like wheat, ³²but I have prayed for you that your faith may not fail; and when you have turned again, strengthen your brethren." ³³And he said to him, "Lord, I am ready to go with you to prison and to death." ³⁴He said, "I tell you, Peter, the cock will not crow this day, until you three times deny that you know me."

35 And he said to them, "When I sent you out with no purse or bag or sandals, did you lack anything?" They said, "Nothing." [36]He said to them, "But now, let him who has a purse take it, and likewise a bag. And let him who has no sword sell his mantle and buy one. [37]For I tell you that this scripture must be fulfilled in me, 'And he was reckoned with transgressors'; for what is written about me has its fulfilment." [38]And they said, "Look, Lord, here are two swords." And he said to them, "It is enough."

39 And he came out, and went, as was his custom, to the Mount of Olives; and the disciples followed him. [40]And when he came to the place he said to them, "Pray that you may not enter into temptation." [41]And he withdrew from them about a stone's throw, and knelt down and prayed, [42]"Father, if thou art willing, remove this cup from me; nevertheless not my will, but thine, be done." [45]And when he rose from prayer, he came to the disciples and found them sleeping for sorrow, [46]and he said to them, "Why do you sleep? Rise and pray that you may not enter into temptation."

47 While he was still speaking, there came a crowd, and the man called Judas, one of the twelve, was leading them. He drew near to Jesus to kiss him; [48]but Jesus said to him, "Judas, would you betray the Son of man with a kiss?" [49]And when those who were about him saw what would follow, they said, "Lord, shall we strike with the sword?" [50]And one of them struck the slave of the high priest and cut off his right ear. [51]But Jesus said, "No more of this!" And he touched his ear and healed him. [52]Then Jesus said to the chief priests and officers of the temple and elders, who had come out against him, "Have you come out as against a robber, with swords and clubs? [53]When I was with you day after day in the temple, you did not lay hands on me. But this is your hour, and the

power of darkness."

54 Then they seized him and led him away, bringing him into the high priest's house. Peter followed at a distance; [55]and when they had kindled a fire in the middle of the courtyard and sat down together, Peter sat among them. [56]Then a maid, seeing him as he sat in the light and gazing at him, said, "This man also was with him." [57]But he denied it, saying, "Woman, I do not know him." [58]And a little later some one else saw him and said, "You also are one of them." But Peter said, "Man, I am not." [59]And after an interval of about an hour still another insisted, saying, "Certainly this man also was with him; for he is a Galilean." [60]But Peter said, "Man, I do not know what you are saying." And immediately, while he was still speaking, the cock crowed. [61]And the Lord turned and looked at Peter. And Peter remembered the word of the Lord, how he had said to him, "Before the cock crows today, you will deny me three times." [62]And he went out and wept bitterly.

63 Now the men who were holding Jesus mocked him and beat him; [64]they also blindfolded him and asked him, "Prophesy! Who is it that struck you?" [65]And they spoke many other words against him, reviling him.

66 When day came, the assembly of the elders of the people gathered together, both chief priests and scribes; and they led him away to their council, and they said, [67]"If you are the Christ, tell us." But he said to them, "If I tell you, you will not believe; [68]and if I ask you, you will not answer. [69]But from now on the Son of man shall be seated at the right hand of the power of God." [70]And they all said, "Are you the Son of God, then?" And he said to them, "You say that I am." [71]And they said, "What further testimony do we need? We have heard it ourselves from his own lips."

looking for a subtle way to get hold of Jesus without having the ordinary people there to witness the capture.

The reader is now aware that he is made the kind of sad spectator who watches two human forces moving through the darkness to collision. Jesus calls for a room in which to celebrate the eating of the lamb and the bread and the drinking of the wine which recalled that last meal his ancestors had as they sprinkled their doorposts and prepared to leave Egypt right after eating. Not everything of Jesus' last supper is told, but rather just those elements of it which Luke finds very meaningful for Theophilus. There is the poignant beginning: Jesus has longed to eat this meal with his friends, for it is his last with them before his lethal suffering. Yet, it is, too, a meal which will be repeated, indeed fulfilled as a prophecy is fulfilled, in the kingdom where they will all be alive and together again in each other's company. The same sentiment is expressed in the drinking of one of the four cups of ritual wine: they drink together from the cup, for they will live again together in the kingdom of God.

Then Jesus takes bread and identifies it as his body given up for his friends. This saying of Jesus is all the more precious since it is so rare that Luke presents Jesus' death as a death for others. He follows with Jesus' words about the wine of the cup, identifying it as Jesus' blood which will be poured out for his friends; moreover, it is a blood which recalls that blood which sealed the covenant God made at an earlier time with Israel. This is the blood which seals the new covenant, which attests to God's willingness to be friends again with human beings. It is not surprising that Jesus asks his friends to re-enact these gestures in his absence, gestures through which his body and blood, in the significance he has here given them, will be present to them.

By this will they remember the significance of his dead body
and spilt blood of tomorrow.

Luke, having pointed up the generous sacrifice of Jesus,
now turns to announcement of the betrayer. The identification of the betrayer seems, however, to be of less interest
at the moment than lessons to be learned from such a subject. First, Scripture has indicated that the Son of Man, before
his glorification, must die, but that obligation does not lessen
the tragic guilt and end of the one who betrays Jesus. Second, there is a lesson to learn from the way Jesus handles
himself: if anyone is a "Lord," it is he, and yet he serves
others, more like a servant than a lord. Third, the reward
for fidelity to Jesus is the kingdom, that very kingdom which
the Father has conferred upon Jesus; thus, faithful disciples
will eat and drink with Jesus at his table—and these twelve
will sit in judgment on the twelve tribes of Israel. In this
the Twelve are unique among Jesus' followers and in a sense
become the successors of those twelve sons of Jacob on
whom Israel of old was founded.

Sharing in the kingdom of Jesus results from fidelity to
him even in his sufferings. This brings up the delicate fact
that Peter will not so much lose faith in Jesus or hand him
over to death, but dissociate himself from his master to
avoid suffering on account of him. Jesus' prayers for him will
be effective in the end, even to the point that Peter will be
a source of strength for the others who will act as he did.

Finally, and in preparation for a time which knows no
physical presence and companionship of Jesus, Jesus speaks
of taking a purse, a haversack, a sword—in short, of preparing to enter a world in which they must survive as followers of a criminal, as Scripture describes Jesus. As often
in semitic speech, it is not the list of concrete details which
is to be taken literally but the situation the speaker is trying

to alert his audience to. Up to now, all have enjoyed the peculiar circumstances and protection that Jesus' physical nearness has provided, as well as the good will of those who could be anticipated to receive the Twelve and the seventy-two on their brief missions. From now on, it will be a different world.

Jesus moves from the southwest corner of Jerusalem to a point outside the northeast corner of the city; it is the other side of the valley which separates Jerusalem from the Mount of Olives. Here Jesus often prayed; here Jesus prayed this night in anguish, for like most every human being, he did not want to die. Luke uses this moment, too, as a lesson. Jesus is being put to the test, and, with God's help, is winning it, as he strives to put here, as elsewhere, the will of God ahead of even his longing to live. As entry and as exit to this personal struggle of Jesus are words to the disciples: you, too, will have your test; pray God that he might spare you from that test of faith.

It is in the garden that Jesus is arrested, for Judas knows where to find Jesus at night. It is by a kiss, the gesture of friendship, that the betrayal is accomplished. The disciples take their cue from Jesus' earlier words and strike with the sword in defense. Jesus did not intend this understanding of his prior words and hastens to cure the man injured by the sword. Two challenges are sent as ringing echoes of the Gospel's pages: Does Jesus deserve to be treated as a criminal? Why was he never apprehended during the daylight when he was visible to all? In any event, it is the hour of darkness, and darkness will have its way.

Peter now fulfills the sad words Jesus had to say about Peter's unwillingness to suffer with him. Three times Peter dissociates himself from Jesus. But at the moment of the third denial, Peter sees his Lord looking straight at him. He is reminded of Jesus' words, of his own assurance of companionship to death, if necessary—and he can only weep, and weep bitterly.

The temple guard (the chief priests, who had authority over all aspects of the temple, including the management of their own temple police or guard) now begin the abuse Jesus had foretold. Luke relates only a small portion of it, out of sympathy.

At first light of morning Jesus is made to face the Sanhedrin, the highest legal authority of Israel. In a few verses Luke has Jesus affirm that his opponents know him to be the Messiah, the Son of Man soon to be seated, as Lord, at God's right hand, as God's Son. That Jesus did not deny these titles, subjects of debate throughout the Gospel, is enough to make the Sanhedrin ask Pilate for Jesus' death, a punishment which they were not allowed to inflict without Roman approval. Before long, it will be the Christian claim that Jesus is to be found, not in death and corruption in the underworld, but seated at the right hand of his Father in power.

23

Jesus on Trial • Jesus Goes to Calvary, Is Crucified, Dies and Is Buried

In presenting Jesus' last supper, agony, and betrayal, mocking and trial, Luke has been schematic; he has not lost the element of sorrow, of grief, but he has preferred to stress parts of these episodes which can do the most good for Theophilus, his reader. Luke continues to tell this sorrowful story in the same manner, not suppressing the anguish and sorrow of these terrible moments but stressing the elements which will most benefit the Christian dedicated to Christ.

The Sanhedrin was a group of seventy men, plus their president, the ruling high priest; this body was constitutionally the equivalent of the judicial, executive and legislative powers rolled into one. Under Roman domination the Sanhedrin still functioned; only in certain matters did Rome restrict the execution of the Sanhedrin's powers. The Sanhedrin was made up of the chief priests, representatives of the scribes and representatives of the elders, or wealthy of Israel. Only to the extent that the members of the Sanhedrin followed the theology and practices of Pharisaism or of Sadduceeism could one say that the Pharisees and Sadducees had influence with the Sanhedrin. In practice, however, it is generally true that the elders and the high and chief priests followed the Saducean theology, that the scribes followed the Pharisean Judaism. The law of Moses was the norm or criterion of judgment, and it was in line with this norm that Jesus was judged by the Sanhedrin; thus, the Sanhedrin was concerned with claims to being the Messiah, Son of God,

23 Then the whole company of them arose, and brought him before Pilate. ²And they began to accuse him, saying, "We found this man perverting our nation, and forbidding us to give tribute to Caesar, and saying that he himself is Christ a king." ³And Pilate asked him, "Are you the King of the Jews?" And he answered him, "You have said so." ⁴And Pilate said to the chief priests and the multitudes, "I find no crime in this man." ⁵But they were urgent, saying, "He stirs up the people, teaching throughout all Judea, from Galilee even to this place."

6 When Pilate heard this, he asked whether the man was a Galilean. ⁷And when he learned that he belonged to Herod's jurisdiction, he sent him over to Herod, who was himself in Jerusalem at that time. ⁸When Herod saw Jesus, he was very glad, for he had long desired to see him, because he had heard about him, and he was hoping to see some sign done by him. ⁹So he questioned him at some length; but he made no answer. ¹⁰The chief priests and the scribes stood by, vehemently accusing him. ¹¹And Herod with his soldiers treated him with contempt and mocked him; then, arraying him in gorgeous apparel, he sent him back to Pilate. ¹²And Herod and Pilate became friends with each other that very day, for before this they had been at enmity with each other.

13 Pilate then called together the chief priests and the rulers and the people, ¹⁴and said to them, "You brought me this man as one who was perverting the people; and after examining him before you, behold, I did not find this man guilty of any of your charges against

him; ¹⁵neither did Herod, for he sent him back to us. Behold, nothing deserving death has been done by him; ¹⁶I will therefore chastise him and release him."

18 But they all cried out together, "Away with this man, and release to us Barabbas"— ¹⁹a man who had been thrown into prison for an insurrection started in the city, and for murder. ²⁰Pilate addressed them once more, desiring to release Jesus; ²¹but they shouted out, "Crucify, crucify him!" ²²A third time he said to them, "Why, what evil has he done? I have found in him no crime deserving death; I will therefore chastise him and release him." ²³But they were urgent, demanding with loud cries that he should be crucified. And their voices prevailed. ²⁴So Pilate gave sentence that their demand should be granted. ²⁵He released the man who had been thrown into prison for insurrection and murder, whom they asked for; but Jesus he delivered up to their will.

26 And as they led him away, they seized one Simon of Cyrene, who was coming in from the country, and laid on him the cross, to carry it behind Jesus. ²⁷And there followed him a great multitude of the people, and of women who bewailed and lamented him. ²⁸But Jesus turning to them said, "Daughters of Jerusalem, do not weep for me, but weep for yourselves and for your children. ²⁹For behold, the days are coming when they will say, 'Blessed are the barren, and the wombs that never bore, and the breasts that never gave suck!' ³⁰Then they will begin to say to the mountains, 'Fall on us'; and to the hills, 'Cover us.' ³¹For if they do this when the wood is green, what will happen when it is dry?"

32 Two others also, who were criminals, were led away to be put to death with him. ³³And when they came to the place which is called The Skull, there they crucified him, and the criminals, one on the right and one on

the left. ³⁴And Jesus said, "Father, forgive them; for they know not what they do." And they cast lots to divide his garments. ³⁵And the people stood by, watching; but the rulers scoffed at him, saying, "He saved others; let him save himself, if he is the Christ of God, his Chosen One!" ³⁶The soldiers also mocked him, coming up and offering him vinegar, ³⁷and saying, "If you are the King of the Jews, save yourself!" ³⁸There was also an inscription over him, "This is the King of the Jews."

39 One of the criminals who were hanged railed at him, saying, "Are you not the Christ? Save yourself and us!" ⁴⁰But the other rebuked him, saying, "Do you not fear God, since you are under the same sentence of condemnation? ⁴¹And we indeed justly; for we are receiving the due reward of our deeds; but this man has done nothing wrong." ⁴²And he said, "Jesus, remember me when you come into your kingdom." ⁴³And he said to him, "Truly, I say to you, today you will be with me in Paradise."

44 It was now about the sixth hour, and there was darkness over the whole land until the ninth hour, ⁴⁵while the sun's light failed; and the curtain of the temple was torn in two. ⁴⁶Then Jesus, crying with a loud voice, said, "Father, into thy hands I commit my spirit!" And having said this he breathed his last. ⁴⁷Now when the centurion saw what had taken place, he praised God, and said, "Certainly this man was innocent!" ⁴⁸And all the multitudes who assembled to see the sight, when they saw what had taken place, returned home beating their breasts. ⁴⁹And all his acquaintances and the women who had followed him from Galilee stood at a distance and saw these things.

50 Now there was a man named Joseph from the Jewish town of Arimathea. He was a member of the

council, a good and righteous man, [51]who had not con-
sented to their purpose and deed, and he was looking for
the kingdom of God. [52]This man went to Pilate and asked
for the body of Jesus. [53]Then he took it down and
wrapped it in a linen shroud, and laid him in a rock-hewn
tomb, where no one had ever yet been laid. [54]It was the
day of Preparation, and the sabbath was beginning. [55]The
women who had come with him from Galilee followed,
and saw the tomb, and how his body was laid; [56]then they
returned, and prepared spices and ointments.

On the sabbath they rested according to the com-
mandment.

Son of Man, Lord of David. However, in bringing Jesus to Roman judges (who alone could send Jesus to death), the accusation or charge must violate Roman law, not necessarily Mosaic law; what would Romans care if Jesus did something which upset Jews, but did not upset Romans?

The Sanhedrin brings Jesus to the Roman authority, now in Jerusalem because of the feast of Passover (usually the Roman authority stayed at Caesarea-by-the-Mediterranean Sea). The Roman authority at this time (26 A.D.–36 A.D.) was Pontius Pilate; his title was procurator, he ruled the territories of Judea and Samaria (as had his Roman predecessors since the year 6 A.D., when Herod the Great's son, Archelaus, had been removed from power because of his harshness), and reported directly to the governor of the Middle East stationed in Damascus. The charge against Jesus is meant to catch Pilate's attention: Jesus incites to riot, opposes payment of taxes to Caesar and claims to be a king (in Jewish terms, Messiah). To Pilate's question "Are you the king of the Jews?" Jesus' answer apparently is enough of a denial that Pilate is moved to say that he finds no guilt in this man on this charge.

The Sanhedrin insists that Jesus' teaching, from Galilee to Jerusalem, has done nothing but incite people to revolt. The mention of Galilee suggests a resolution of this argument, at least for Pilate. Pilate does not rule Galilee; the son of Herod the Great, Antipas, has ruled Galilee since 4 B.C. and, like Pilate, has come to Jerusalem for the feast. Why not let Herod Antipas make the decision?

The sum and substance of Jesus' trial before Antipas was ridicule and contempt of the prisoner; at least, however, the eagerness Luke had reported earlier about Herod Antipas' desire to meet this Jesus had been slaked, and through this sharing of the prisoner Herod and Pilate finally became friends.

Now Jesus is back in Pilate's hands. He persists in his judgment of Jesus' innocence, supported by Herod, and offers the compromise of a flogging, justified apparently because Jesus has disturbed the peace. Indeed, three times does Pilate insist that Jesus is innocent, certainly not guilty of death, particularly not deserving of the crucifixion everyone now asks for. Luke has, within the brief space allotted to him, established the innocence of Jesus in the eyes of those who have no ax to grind, no prejudice. Pilate now gives Jesus into their hands, to do with him as they please, while allowing a certain Barabbas (a cause of riot and a murderer) to go free; Luke presumes that the crowd has had a choice, and that they prefer a man like Barabbas to a man like Jesus. A reflection on the irony of this detail, as of others, will occur in the Acts of the Apostles.

Jesus' walk to the crucifixion place (about three quarters of a mile) includes three details. Simon from Cyrene in Africa is made to carry what Jesus can no longer carry, the cross-bar of his cross. According to Roman law, a soldier could force anyone to help him carry things for a mile, as long as the soldier was on duty. Second, to women who often tried to give comfort to prisoners like Jesus, Jesus can only turn their attention from his fate, grievous as it is, to the terrible fate in store for the Jerusalem which is rejecting him. If Jerusalem acts this way now, how will it act when it is put to suffering? Third, we learn that two others are being led out to crucifixion, like Jesus.

At the place called the Skull (or Calvary), an abandoned quarry and an area in which were graves (visible even today) and some sparse grass—just outside the northwestern gate of Jerusalem—Jesus is crucified between the other two people, criminals like himself.

Jesus' first reported act is an intervention with his Father, asking forgiveness for his opponents, since they do not know what they are doing; this ignorance will be referred to again in Acts 3. The clothes of Jesus are to be won by the casting of lots, surely a reference to Psalm 22 (cf. v 18) in which so many of the details of the crucifixion are mirrored (cf. also Psalm 69: 21: "They gave me vinegar...").

Above Jesus was written the charge justifying his crucifixion: King of the Jews. Incited by sight of this, the Jewish leaders, the soldiers, and one of the criminals shout to Jesus, derisively, to let his kingship show by an exercise of his power: free yourself. Indeed, he saved others—and if he is from God, where is God now? One of the criminals underlines Jesus' innocence, accepts his own punishment as just, but calls on Jesus as Messiah, to bring him into Jesus' kingdom. This request for mercy, as with every other request, is granted immediately; indeed, the criminal will pass from death to paradise, to be with Jesus.

Jesus now dies, enveloped in the darkness, for it is, as he said, the hour of darkness, from noon to 3:00 P.M. The veil of the temple, which separated the holiest place on earth from all human beings (except the high priest who, once a year, was allowed to enter the Holy of Holies to ask for the forgiveness of Israel's sins of that year), is completely torn, so that all people can have access to God, so that God's mercy may extend to all men; the old form of seeking forgiveness is now replaced through the death of Jesus. Jesus cites a psalm (Ps 31:5) of trust in his Father, and expires.

It is not altogether clear what moves the centurion to praise God and confess that Jesus was a great and good man; perhaps it was his trust in God as his Father, and the care he had for the repentant criminal rather than for himself, and his prayer of intercession to ward off punishment of his enemies. In any event, at least one admits Jesus' innocence and uprightness, and it is clearly significant that he was a pagan. In fact, many of the people who had been a part of the condemning crowd now return home gesturing their regrets.

Jesus' friends, the future witnesses to all aspects of Jesus' time on earth, particularly the women first mentioned in Lk 8:1—3—these note all that happened and, thereafter, where Jesus was buried. The women, who had not time to care for the body properly before the sabbath began (6:00 P.M.), also noted the exact tomb into which Jesus had been placed by Joseph from Arimathea in Israel, and the very position of the body; by underlining the eye-witnessing of these people Luke is already preparing for their witnessing on behalf of the resurrection of Jesus from the dead.

24

*Jesus Risen • The Disciples' Future Described •
Jesus Ascends to His Father • The Disciples
Await His Gift*

If I were true to Luke's way of thinking, I would not start this comment with a capital letter, nor with a new chapter heading, for the resurrection of Jesus is supposed to flow smoothly right out of his death and burial; the resurrection is not a new chapter, but the next moment after entombment.

It is the first day of the week; this note suggests that we get our timing straight. At the time of Jesus a day began at what is for us 6:00 P.M., instead of at our midnight. Thus, Jesus died about 3:00 P.M., just three hours before a new day, according to calculation of the time. This new day was, by coincidence, a sabbath day (= Saturday), a day which ended at 6:00 P.M. on Saturday, a day on which the work of anointing a body was forbidden. As of 6:00 P.M. a new day began, Sunday, which was, according to the days of creation in Genesis, the first day of the week (recall that God had rested at the end of six days of creating, and this day of rest is the sabbath). Since the first twelve or so hours of this new day, Sunday, were in darkness, the women waited till sunrise of Sunday to go to the tomb to finish what they had begun in the last hours of Friday.

It is the women who followed Jesus from Galilee who come to the tomb, who actually go into the tomb—to find that the body of Jesus is gone; it is these very women who

SCRIPTURE TEXT

24 But on the first day of the week, at early dawn, they went to the tomb, taking the spices which they had prepared. ²And they found the stone rolled away from the tomb, ³but when they went in they did not find the body. ⁴While they were perplexed about this, behold, two men stood by them in dazzling apparel; ⁵and as they were frightened and bowed their faces to the ground, the men said to them, "Why do you seek the living among the dead? ⁶Remember how he told you, while he was still in Galilee, ⁷that the Son of man must be delivered into the hands of sinful men, and be crucified, and on the third day rise." ⁸And they remembered his words, ⁹and returning from the tomb they told all this to the eleven and to all the rest. ¹⁰Now it was Mary Magdalene and Joanna and Mary the mother of James and the other women with them who told this to the apostles; ¹¹but these words seemed to them an idle tale, and they did not believe them.

13 That very day two of them were going to a village named Emmaus, about seven miles from Jerusalem, ¹⁴and talking with each other about all these things that had happened. ¹⁵While they were talking and discussing together, Jesus himself drew near and went with them. ¹⁶But their eyes were kept from recognizing him. ¹⁷And he said to them, "What is this conversation which you are holding with each other as you walk?" And they stood still, looking sad. ¹⁸Then one of them, named Cleopas, answered him, "Are you the only visitor to Jerusalem who does not know the things that have happened there in these days?" ¹⁹And he said to them, "What things?" And

they said to him, "Concerning Jesus of Nazareth, who was a prophet mighty in deed and word before God and all the people, [20]and how our chief priests and rulers delivered him up to be condemned to death, and crucified him. [21]But we had hoped that he was the one to redeem Israel. Yes, and besides all this, it is now the third day since this happened. [22]Moreover, some women of our company amazed us. They were at the tomb early in the morning [23]and did not find his body; and they came back saying that they had even seen a vision of angels, who said that he was alive. [24]Some of those who were with us went to the tomb, and found it just as the women had said; but him they did not see." [25]And he said to them, "O foolish men, and slow of heart to believe all that the prophets have spoken! [26]Was it not necessary that the Christ should suffer these things and enter into his glory?" [27]And beginning with Moses and all the prophets, he interpreted to them in all the scriptures the things concerning himself.

28 So they drew near to the village to which they were going. He appeared to be going further, [29]but they constrained him, saying, "Stay with us, for it is toward evening and the day is now far spent." So he went in to stay with them. [30]When he was at table with them, he took the bread and blessed, and broke it, and gave it to them. [31]And their eyes were opened and they recognized him; and he vanished out of their sight. [32]They said to each other, "Did not our hearts burn within us while he talked to us on the road, while he opened to us the scriptures?" [33]And they rose that same hour and returned to Jerusalem; and they found the eleven gathered together and those who were with them, [34]who said, "The Lord has risen indeed, and has appeared to Simon!" [35]Then

they told what had happened on the road, and how he was known to them in the breaking of the bread.

36 As they were saying this, Jesus himself stood among them. [37]But they were startled and frightened, and supposed that they saw a spirit. [38]And he said to them, "Why are you troubled, and why do questionings rise in your hearts? [39]See my hands and my feet, that it is I myself; handle me, and see; for a spirit has not flesh and bones as you see that I have." [41]And while they still disbelieved for joy, and wondered, he said to them, "Have you anything here to eat?" [42]They gave him a piece of broiled fish, [43]and he took it and ate before them.

44 Then he said to them, "These are my words which I spoke to you, while I was still with you, that everything written about me in the law of Moses and the prophets and the psalms must be fulfilled." [45]Then he opened their minds to understand the scriptures, [46]and said to them, "Thus it is written, that the Christ should suffer and on the third day rise from the dead, [47]and that repentance and forgiveness of sins should be preached in his name to all nations, beginning from Jerusalem. [48]You are witnesses of these things. [49]And behold, I send the promise of my Father upon you; but stay in the city, until you are clothed with power from on high."

50 Then he led them out as far as Bethany, and lifting up his hands he blessed them. [51]While he blessed them, he parted from them, and was carried up into heaven. [52]And they returned to Jerusalem with great joy, [53]and were continually in the temple blessing God.

had marked the tomb and the exact position of the body—eye-witnesses.

The story Luke tells does not describe the rising of Jesus to life. Luke's story is meant to underline another facet, namely, the questionableness of coming to Jesus' tomb with ointments and spices, as though he were expected to be found still dead. Why expect to find him dead? The divine messengers are meant to announce both the fact that he has already risen and that his death and resurrection should both have been expected: he had already in Galilee affirmed the necessity of his death and resurrection, and that the death and resurrection was to be understood as that of the Son of Man. The reader, like the women, now remembers Jesus' words.

The women now become messengers or witnesses; the Eleven and all the others, who eventually will preach the resurrection of Jesus, do not believe. Peter takes it upon himself to check at least the silent fact of the empty tomb; his confirmation of an empty tomb leaves him amazed at what has happened, but we are not sure that he yet believes that Jesus has risen. The empty tomb does not produce faith; the eye-witness experience of Jesus does.

Two of those to whom the women spoke of their experience are leaving Jerusalem for their home in Emmaus, northwest of Jerusalem. With an element of story-telling made famous by Greek tragedians and other ancient literary figures, Luke has Jesus come up alongside these two disciples without their realizing who he actually is. Jesus' question about their discussion between themselves as they leave Jerusalem's gates results in a very good summary of the Gospel story Luke has portrayed since Jesus' return from the desert after his baptism. All the essential data is here, except for two points; understanding and experience of the risen Jesus. These two points are now addressed. Without reference to specific texts, Jesus so explains the Scriptures to these two that the life of Jesus and the necessity of his death and resurrection make sense: "their hearts were burning." Jesus agrees to stay with them and settles down to supper with them. While at supper, he so took the bread and wine, so blessed it and gave it to them, that they suddenly recognized him; they realize that he lives, that they have met the risen Jesus. With this experience of the risen Jesus they believe. Many interpreters think that Luke's distinction between understanding Jesus' life through the Scriptures and knowing the risen Jesus through the blessed bread and wine is meant to encourage Theophilus in his celebration of the Eucharist: through the reading of Scripture Theophilus will understand Jesus; through the blessing of the bread and wine Theophilus will live with the risen Jesus. According to this second resurrection episode, Scripture has shown that the anointed successor of David had to die and had to rise in order to reach his throne.

With the return of these two disciples to Jerusalem we learn of an appearance of Jesus to Peter which Luke does not describe. Such appearances are what lead directly to belief.

Now there is granted to everyone an experience of the risen Jesus. In this meeting Jesus calls on all to touch him and look carefully at him, and he even eats something. He does this with a view to their being able to witness that he is truly risen. More precisely, he does this because they had, according to the story, thought they were seeing a ghost or phantom at first. Luke does not want the risen Jesus confused with spirits or ghosts or phantoms, nor is Jesus risen just a less-than-human representation of himself, as people of this time often imagined the dead to be. Jesus was fully himself; what is risen is what had lived and died—it is all one and the same. Not only does this insistence help toward understanding the Jesus who now lives; Jesus opens the minds of all to understand all that the Scriptures had said would happen to a person Jesus identifies as himself, then as the Davidic Anointed one (= Christ). It all had to happen to whoever was the Christ.

Three times Luke has had recourse to past prophecies to explain the necessity of death and the necessity of resurrection. Now he adds another stage in the elements of this long-standing necessity; the Scriptures, which voice the plan of God, speak of the preaching of repentance in Jesus' name, after his being raised from the dead. This is a preaching which will begin in, of all places, Jerusalem which has killed the prophets; it is a preaching at the heart of which is witness to all that has happened, especially to the resurrection of Jesus. For unless Jesus lived after his death, why would anyone think Jesus would be a central, pivotal element in repentance and forgiveness—he would be dead, clearly impotent!

The disciples are to receive soon the Holy Spirit of God, but Luke does not use the words "Holy Spirit." He prefers to have the reader understand, even before the second volume begins, that the Spirit of God is a promise of the Father to Israel; thus, the Pentecost is also a fulfillment of God's Scriptures. But not only is the Spirit of God to be considered as a promise of the Father; the Spirit's coming is to be understood as a "clothing in power from on high." Attention is drawn specifically to the strength and energy the Spirit will give to those who should witness, who should speak on behalf of God. We will see how all this takes place in the next volume, but it should be clear that, at this juncture of his work, Luke is at the same time moving away from showing that only the death and resurrection of Jesus was prophesied and looking forward to the mission of witnessing to repentance in the name of Jesus for the forgiveness of sins.

Luke closes this volume with Jesus' blessing of his disciples and his Father's taking Jesus up to himself. Jesus had set out for Jerusalem as the days for his being taken up were about to happen; they have happened. The disciples worship Jesus, a sign of their recognition of his intimate relationship with Yahweh, of his kingship. They also return to Jerusalem with joy, for Jesus' ending is a glorious, befitting one. Where else should they all be found but where the book began— in the temple of God, in praise of him, for all that he has brought to pass. The volume is ended, but not the story.

Conclusion

The Jewish Scriptures had foretold the coming of Yahweh's Kingdom. The divine witness and the power of Jesus suggest that Jesus is the Messiah who inaugurates this Kingdom. Surprising as it may be, this Messiah not only "had" to begin the Kingdom, but he also "had" to die. The Kingdom, then, is begun in a peculiar way, for it did not reach its completion in the life of Jesus, nor has it reached its fulfillment in the life of Jesus's witnesses. Jesus's death was followed by resurrection, an entry for Jesus into "the age to come." His followers, however, remained in "this age," with the result that, though some of the characteristics which belong to the Kingdom of God are felt by believers, many of the characteristics of "this age" are still characteristics of their lives. Experiences, interpreted by the guidance of God's own Spirit, helped the early Christians to realize both the Messiahship of Jesus and the partial entrance of God's Kingdom into their world. Luke, like others, began to see that Jesus was the good news of God, but that the good news of God had to be given to all mankind; thus, there was a plan of God extending beyond the time and place of Palestine in 30 A.D. extending for as long as God desired.

Jesus, then, has returned to the right hand of his Father, as God had already determined he would; the plan of salvation, however, with Jesus at its dynamic center, is still

looking to be completed. With great gratitude we have stud-
ied the life of Jesus as Luke gave it to us; now we look
forward to seeing the completion of Jesus' mission, as Luke
has invited us to see it, in Luke's second and final volume.
The Gospel has given us the invaluable teachings, deeds and
character of Jesus; let us see how all this is transmitted faithfully to the ends of the earth.

Bibliography for Further Reading, Study and Reflection

THE GOSPEL OF LUKE

Caird, G. *St. Luke.* Philadelphia: Westminster, 1978.

Danker, F. *Luke.* Philadelphia: Fortress Press, 1976. (Proclamation Series)

Fitzmyer, J. *The Gospel according to Luke.* Garden City: Doubleday, 1981, 1985. (Anchor Bible, vols. 28 & 28a)

Harrington, W. *The Gospel of St. Luke.* Westminster: Newman Press, 1967.

Karris, R. *Invitation to Luke.* Garden City: Image Books, 1977.

Kealy, S. *The Gospel of Luke.* Denville: Dimension, 1979.

Kodell, J. *The Gospel according to Luke.* Collegeville: Liturgical Press, 1983.

LaVerdiere, E. *Luke.* Wilmington: Glazier, 1980.

Schweizer, E. *The Good News according to Luke.* Atlanta: John Knox, 1984.

LUKE'S GOSPEL AND ACTS OF THE APOSTLES

Juel, D. *Luke-Acts: The Promise of History.* Atlanta: John Knox, 1983.

Karris, R. *What Are They Saying About Luke and Acts?* Mahwah: Paulist Press, 1979.

Kurz, W. *Following Jesus: A Disciple's Guide to Luke and Acts.* Ann Arbor: Servant Books, 1984.

Maddox, R. *The Purpose of Luke-Acts.* Edinburgh: T. & T. Clark, 1982.

O'Toole, R. *The Unity of Luke's Theology.* Wilmington: Glazier, 1984.

Van Linden, P. *The Gospel of Luke and Acts.* Wilmington: Glazier, 1986.